Forty Years In Preschool

Sudie Doughton Mason

*For Peg
Much love,
Sudie*

For Pat,
Much love,
[signature]

Contents

Part I   1
Children I Have Known

Part II   35
Subjects Dear to My Heart

Part III   109
My Education to Become a Teacher

Part IV   119
First Job - Sweet Memorial Day Care in Chile

Part V   135
Graduate School, University Teaching,
Parent Co-op, Head Start

Part VI   149
Montessori Work

Part VII   213
Bibliography

Important Note and Disclaimer: Due to the many people who have influenced me and my own propensity to integrate and change slightly as I go, differences or errors in my interpretation of Montessori's ideas or of those of other authors and educators should be attributed to me solely and not to any particular school or other individual.

Copyright © 2007 Sudie Doughton Mason
All rights reserved.
ISBN: 1-4196-6587-1
ISBN-13: 978-1419665875

Visit www.booksurge.com to order additional copies.

About the Author

I was born in North Carolina in 1937. I have fond memories of growing up in a colorful and interesting family. My connections to the "Tar Heel State" continue to be strong because many members of my family still live there. I try to visit once a year.

North Carolina, Chile, Tennessee, Montana, and Washington (state) have all been "home" at different times in my life. In the last twenty years we have spent most summers in British Columbia, Canada. Each setting has given me unique experiences, many friends, and lots of challenges.

My marriage in 1965 brought with it four energetic and vibrant children. Now we have six grandchildren and eleven great-grand children!

My interests, other than family, religion, and education include: kayaking, boating in general, nature, healthy foods, hiking, arts and crafts, languages, and other cultures.

Now approaching "three score and ten," I feel grateful to have been a part of so many interesting adventures and to have known so many wonderful people. Hopefully there will be an adventure or two still awaiting me.

Sudie Doughton Mason

Preface

This book is not a text book or a research paper. It is more like a patchwork quilt or collage about my career in Early Childhood, the people who influenced it the most, and my resulting thoughts about what is important in teaching young children. Most of my work was focused on children who were three, four, and five years of age. Most of my advice has to do with those ages. I loved the children's art work, their spontaneity, love of life, their points of view, their honesty, and the incredible uniqueness of each child.

The subjects that one can discuss in the area of Early Childhood are indeed broad and deep. They concern issues of general human development as well as specific methods of teaching and learning. Although these subjects are often intertwined in inseparable ways, they do have different etiologies and different major emphases. Most of my early work was grounded in theories of human development, and the second half of my career was spent in studying the philosophy and applying the educational theories and practices of Maria Montessori.

My three years in Chile working at a Methodist Day Care Center was the beginning of my formal work with young children. After that there was graduate school at the University of Tennessee, two years teaching at UT, ten years at the University of Montana, two years teaching in a Peninsula College Co-Op Preschool, four years in Head Start, and about fifteen at Montessori Community School in Port Angeles, Washington.

After I retired from regular work, for two or three years, I volunteered once a week in a local school to help children with reading and to read stories in a kindergarten class. I gave workshops at many conferences sponsored by our Olympic Peninsula Association of Young Children. I tutored children at my home and worked part-time in a day care home. In both of those last settings, I tried to use some of the Montessori teaching strategies.

Writing takes on a life of its own. When I read what I have written and reflect on it, I often have new insights about a child or a situation, a theory, or even about myself. It is rather exciting, yet also humbling to see something in a new light. I have tried to mention these thoughts when appropriate. It has also made writing more interesting than I had thought it would be.

I owe a debt to my husband, Bill and the children, Linda, Clifford, Lucky, and Janet. Over the years, they all added spark, support, and love to my life, and they certainly gave me insights no book had taught me. Indeed, their presence, their ideas, their needs, and interests often made me question some of my cherished assumptions and beliefs just as my father's daily comments with many different points of view had kept me questioning and thinking during my growing-up years.

Each section of *Forty Years in Preschool* has its own dedication and foreword. My thanks go out to all the people who have been a part of my life. Our lives truly extend and interweave with those of our family, friends, students, and all our teachers in whatever guises they appear. Of course, among my teachers were many authors and the books they wrote. Reading the bibliography might be a good place to start! Best wishes.

SDM

Acknowledgments

Many people have helped in getting this book together. Bill, my husband, spent hours solving the technical problems with the computer. He helped me prepare the book in the right format for the publishers.

Kevin Mason, Bill's first cousin, drove over from Port Townsend to photograph the children's artwork for the cover. Thanks to him for a marvelous job in both taking the pictures and in photo editing.

Susan Lynch-Ritchie, a professional in Early Childhood and a good friend for thirty years, was one of the first people to see the original material for this book. It was a haphazard collection of papers that I had written on the boat one summer. She asked the question of who was my intended audience. So I thought about that and I tried to clarify who my readers might be for various sections of the book. In so doing I became more conscious of things to include and things to delete.

Several people read bits and pieces from Part II as I finished editing them. Janet, my daughter, was enthusiastic. She especially liked the paper on the "Importance of Singing." She gave me some of her own ideas on the "Face of the Teacher" which made me rethink and rewrite part of that selection.

Penney Sanders-Thiemann, my "new" neighbor and "a renowned educator," read Part I after I thought I had finished that section. I had written more extensively about some children than others. She suggested I add more information to the shorter vignettes. I have done that. Penney has often been a sounding board for my thoughts and questions concerning some of the ideas I wrote about. She has shared coffee and laughter and helped me stay on course.

Betty Nicholson, my friend and mentor, spent hours with me going over Part VI about our work in Montessori Community School. She agreed with most of my memories and applauded my efforts to describe our school. I was thankful she remembered a few things I had forgotten!

Elsa Johnson, a friend and Montessori teacher who has expertise in writing, read my completed document and made suggestions as to punctuation, sentence formation, etc. She also discussed with me paragraphs which might have been confusing or difficult to understand and we worked together to improve them.

Many of the parents of our former Montessori children have been a source of support and encouragement through the years. Without their continued belief in the value of the Montessori program, I do not think I would have written this book. Special thanks to Linda Pisciotta, Rosanna Yates-Bailey, and Mike Doherty who have continued to give me articles about Montessori, share the art work of their children, and talk with me about the significance of Montessori education in the lives of their children. Katherine Godbey, another Montessori parent, deserves special thanks for the years she served as treasurer for our school (without financial remuneration!)

The paintings and drawings on the front cover were from a variety of sources. Three of the large crayon drawings were among children's work I brought back with me from Chile. Several drawings were made by children in my mother's first-grade class in the late 1920s; our own children did four of the pictures in the mid-1960s; several marker/paintings were shared with me by "Montessori parents" who had saved work from home as well as school; the rest were from my own collection, which includes pictures and paintings from children in many of the places where I worked and/or volunteered. Thanks to all the children who drew and painted and to all the adults who saved the work!

Part I
Children I Have Known

In memory of **Margaret Houser Becker**

    I first met Peggy (Margaret) Becker at the large Methodist Day Care Center in Santiago, Chile, where I began my career in 1960. She and her husband, Max, a forester with the U.S. Agency for International Development program, had been in Chile several years before I arrived. Peggy had worked diligently to set up a "state of the art preschool" for the morning program at this day care center, which was a part of Sweet Memorial Institute. She taught the staff there how to work with children in a "choice type" program, and she taught me too since I was a relative novice having had only three undergraduate courses in Child Development.
    Everywhere Peggy went with her husband in various assignments around the world, she worked with young children and their families. She not only loved people and children in particular, but she was a careful observer of each time and place and she constantly questioned and thought about what she observed and what she was trying to accomplish.

Sudie Doughton Mason

I treasure all the hours we spent together talking about our work at Sweet and life in general. Her home was always open to me, and she and Max were like "stand-in" parents in my three years in Chile. I appreciate the encouragement she gave me to continue my studies in the field of Early Childhood.

Peggy could brighten any day. If she came to volunteer at Sweet or just to visit awhile, I think everyone on the staff was encouraged and happy. "Sra. Becker is here," one girl would say to the next with a smile on her face. If for some reason I was in my own room (I lived at Sweet as did many people who worked there) and looked down and out the windows and saw her blue Chevy pull up and park, my heart would sing.

Below is a favorite poem that Peggy shared with me. I printed it out in black India ink and had it on the door to my office at the University of Tennessee circa 1965.

> "I saw tomorrow marching by on many children's feet,
> And in their forms and faces read her prophesy complete.
> I saw tomorrow look at me through many children's eyes,
> And I thought, how carefully we would teach, if we were only wise."
> Author unknown

After our years together in Chile, we kept up our friendship through letters, telephone calls, and occasional visits. In later years, Peggy did not share my enthusiasm for Montessori, and she never hesitated to say so if I brought up the subject. But that did not dampen our love and friendship.

Peggy continued to work at causes she believed in all her life. Even in her eighties she was still busy leading many programs about other countries and missions of The United Methodist Church. Her Christmas letters, which brought me up to date on her and Max's activities, also brought news from the lives of their children, grandchildren, and great-grandchildren!

Peggy left us for "higher ground" on January 12, 2006. I wish she could have read the stories about the little children in this part of my book. She would have felt empathy for each child. I will not forget her friendship and love and the many things she taught me.

Children I Have Known

Note: Peggy and Max's younger daughter, Marilyn Peters, has recently published a devotional book, *Paw Prints of the Tiger*. It includes wonderful adventure stories from the lives of her missionary grandparents, her parents, and her own family of present. See bibliography for more information.

Foreword

Although the following write-ups are based on real children and real happenings, I have changed the names of the children in most cases. For the purposes of this book, time and space dictate that I mention just a few of the hundreds of children I have known. I did choose to tell about experiences with children that seemed to teach me something…something that I consciously carried with me from that time on. Hopefully what I gleaned from them may be helpful to others. The first piece about Maria was from my first place of work, but the rest of the children are not in the order that I knew them.

MARIA, THE SILENT, EXPRESSIONLESS CHILD

Maria was a frail two-year-old in the Sweet Memorial Day Care Center where I worked in Santiago, Chile, in the early '60s. She sat in the toddler room, looking down at the floor, and not responding to any of the movement of the other children playing in the room. She was thin and blond so she stood out easily from all the other children by her physical appearance as well as her lack of activity.

Her brother, in the classroom for the three- through six-year-olds, played and participated in all the activities. He seemed like a "normal" and competent four-year-old. He already spoke Spanish well. The children belonged to a European family that had immigrated to Chile two or three years previously. The father had recently abandoned the family. Communication with the mother was difficult for us, as her Spanish and English were poor. I knew nothing of Maria's development in infancy.

I observed Maria from time to time, and occasionally I tried to elicit some reaction from her. She stared ahead or looked at the floor. Although she could walk and feed herself, these seemed to be the only things she did like the other children. However, the adults treated her in much the same manner as they did all the children. She was given hugs and greetings upon arrival. She was washed and changed into day care center uniforms. All the washing, changing of clothes, etc. meant that the children got a certain amount of individual attention with the warmth and touch of the personnel who seemed to enjoy the children. But there was more than enjoyment…it was like a mutual attachment between the children and workers. The children were at the center about ten hours a day, five days a week, and a half-day on Sat. for eleven months of the year.

When Maria turned three she was sent over to the room for children aged three through six where her brother was. There were about fifty children in that room. For activities, the children were divided into two groups and the groups took turns playing outside or doing inside activities. For meals and nap time all fifty children were in this large room. I worked in that room daily so I had opportunity to observe Maria each day. Her brother did not seem to pay her much attention. He just went about playing with his friends. I never saw her approach him and seek his attention in any way. In that room, Maria showed the same expressionless face, but she did walk around some and she did follow routines like getting up to go outside, sitting in a chair at the big circle time, etc.

There was one other little blond girl in the class who was probably a little older than Maria. She seemed to like Maria. She would sit next to her at meals or at group. She would stroke her hair and take her by the hand. Maria let her do this. The friend would take her by the hand and lead her to the dramatic play area and Maria would just sit and stare while the others played. Over the next year Maria began to show some eye contact and slight expressions when she was with her friend. Then there was the occasional word. Gradually in the next year she began to interact with that child and then with other children. She began to talk a little. Last of all she began to respond to an adult's communication with her. I had watched Maria during the three-year period of time that I worked at Sweet Memorial.

Children I Have Known

When I left Chile, she was five years old and still in the "three through six" section of the day care center. Although she had not yet become talkative, spontaneous, and openly affectionate like the majority of the Chilean children, her progress was remarkable.

Comments and Thoughts

A child may spontaneously contribute greatly to another child's improvement. Certainly it seemed so in this instance. It is interesting to wonder if the similar hair color of the two girls fostered the relationship in some way.

I believe that the **consistent, predictable, attentive** care given by the adults at the center also played a significant part in Maria's overall well-being and progress. In general she was treated just as one of the group.

In the three-to-six class, she would go to wash for lunch or walk outside when the group went out to play or march in a circle at rhythm time. She fed herself. The program we were using did not require individual work on the part of the child. There were many opportunities to use puzzles, crayons and paints, blocks, books, etc. Maria took little or no observable interest in any of those things. It was only in writing this up recently that the remembrance of her following the routine by physically moving from one place to the next occurred to me as significant. My initial observations of her must have focused more on what she was not doing than on what she was doing!

Also it is interesting to note that there was no planned, agreed upon intervention or overt trying to change her by the teachers. I do not mean to imply that planned, active intervention is not needed in many situations. And of course there had been someone's planned intervention that made it possible for Maria and her brother to attend this center.

Maria did nothing at the center that upset the adults or other children. Consequently people were not wary of her or disliking of her. The staff was not worn out with her as is sometimes the way adults feel with difficult children or children who are failing to meet goals set up for them.

And of what importance is staying in the same day care situation many years, assuming it is a good care center? This child as most others at Sweet entered the same building each morning and had the same caring adults and same children around her for most of the first five or six years of her life. I'm not actually sure how old she was when she came to Sweet.

Maria's changes happened very, very slowly. We live in a culture that is fast-paced, and most of us are uneasy with slow. But the direction we are moving in is important. Slow may be a reasonable and doable speed for many of us in various situations.

BRADLEY AND "THE REAL WORK" OF THE CHILD

Bradley began coming to our Montessori class when he was three. He was an energetic child and he already had lots of ideas about what he wanted to do. One day early in the school year, he went to the easel and he painted or drew the outline of a large dinosaur. He took that down, got an older child to help him put up another sheet of paper, and made a slightly different dinosaur. When he finished the second outline he took it off the easel and went to get another sheet of paper. I glanced up and then I got up and went over to remind him of the "two sheets a day" rule and to suggest that he could paint the dinosaurs he had already made.

He told me in a confident yet friendly way that he did not want to do that. He said he wanted to make lots of dinosaurs. I hesitated for a moment trying to figure out the best way to handle the situation. Suddenly I had an idea…old newspaper didn't have to be limited. It was not in the category of clean sheets of paper for painting and drawing. "Sure, let me get some newspaper from the closet and you can make all you want," I said. Happily, he began drawing large dinosaurs on the old newspaper. The print on the newspaper did not deter him in any way. He concentrated for a long time on his chosen work. He cut each one of them out. When he went home he had a great menagerie.

Comments and Thoughts

It is important to observe each child to see what the real work is that the child is doing. In this case it was drawing large outlines of lots of dinosaurs and cutting them out. By "thinking outside the box" for moment, I was able to maintain the rules and still meet the child's needs.

Children I Have Known

The fact that Bradley talked with me in a confident, yet friendly voice, probably at some level trusting that this situation would turn out OK, helped me as a teacher to look further and think more. By his tone of voice and body language I knew he was not challenging my authority nor was he being demanding or "falling apart." So the situation was not complicated by difficult behavior.

There was a reason for my general rule about easel paper. I had discovered over the years that children were usually more creative, careful, and resourceful if the paper supply was limited. I also was aware in this situation that it was early in the year and I was trying to establish the basic guidelines for activities in the classroom with the new children. I did not want to make an exception to the rule before the guideline was firmly established in the minds of the children.

In one of the first Child Development classes I ever took, I had learned that we need to give with a cheerful spirit. If it is impossible to give a child what they ask for, we may need to say no, but if we are going to say yes, then we need to do it gladly and not grudgingly. So I was happy to give him the newspapers and tell him to make all he wanted.

Probably many of you have wondered at the "dinosaurs" since most three-year-olds do not make recognizable pictures. This child had many gifts. It wasn't long before I heard him match the sounds of the Montessori bells with ease. He did not need to spend as much time as most children matching a smaller number first. He also seemed to understand, use, and master with ease most of our other sensorial equipment after having had it demonstrated by the teacher. By midyear of his first year in Montessori, he knew and understood what all the numbers from 1 to 10 meant. Soon after that he began to devour the letters remembering easily from day to day the sounds he had learned before. The following year he went through our complete reading program and was a good reader by the end of that year. This was also unusual for a four-year-old.

I had a belief in the importance of each child moving at his own rate. It was exciting and interesting to have this child for a student. But I tried outwardly to treat him just like everyone else. In our school we tried to follow the principle of not giving much overt praise or criticism. We wanted the children to recognize an inner satisfaction from work. Bradley had arrived at our school with the mastery of that goal pretty much in hand.

DEBBIE AND CHILDREN'S IDEAS ABOUT THEMSELVES

Debbie was a smart, articulate five-year-old in my kindergarten class at the Univ. of Tennessee. She disliked everything connected with creative art work. "I can't do it," she would complain. She stayed away from the paper and crayons and paints as much as possible. Nothing I tried or said seemed to help her relax and enjoy creating until our experience on the day of a snowfall. That day, I got out some grey paper and some blue paper (choices for the background) and chalk to use with the crayons. I suggested that the children make a picture of the snow and add themselves, friends or a snowman, as they liked.

Most of the children were drawing their pictures and as usual Debbie wiggled in her chair, held the crayon, and looked miserable. She said to me that she knew she would not like whatever she drew. I accepted her comment nonchalantly. Then it occurred to me that maybe not having to draw, but rather cutting out things to paste down for her picture might work for her. I suggested this and I told her that she could use some small pieces of construction paper and cut out her pieces. That way she could look over anything she made before she pasted it down. If she didn't like it, she could cut out something else and try again.

She chose a blue paper for the background. She proceeded to cut little white pieces to be the snow falling and then some big white circular figures for a snowman. She arranged them first one way and then another and when she got the things she wanted just the way she wanted them she glued it all down. After this success, Debbie would choose occasionally to make a collage at activity time. Eventually she tried painting at the easel, and finally she began to draw with crayons.

Comments and Thoughts

I learned from Debbie that becoming successful in a way that made sense to her was necessary before she could begin to change. The fact that I did not have a plan for exactly how her picture should look and I believed in her ability to draw or make something with her own imagination made no sense to her. As a vivacious and smart five-year-old, she had already formed her own ideas about what she was "good at" and "bad at."

If children have announced by words or body language that they will fail at some activity, then in order to maintain their own idea of who they are, they will have to fail at the activity. There seems to be an internal monitoring system in us that wants to keep us steady and true to what we believe. This is a good thing in many instances, but it does make it hard for us to accept new ideas about our abilities and make the efforts to change. If a child has a "block" in some activity, it may help to suggest to the child a similar activity rather than proceeding with the more stressful one. This worked in this case.

Debbie had some strong suits. One was that she was confidant enough to speak her mind and share her thoughts and fears with adults. This meant that now and in the future, she would engage her parents and her teachers in the quest to make sense of things, to share her own ideas, and to get help if needed. This is an important ability for a child to develop. As adults, our reactions to a child's ideas and concerns may encourage the child to speak out or may stifle them from doing so.

Trying to fathom why this child felt so negatively about her creative art work was not as important to me as trying to help her get another point of view. Sometimes I think as adults who work with children we get stymied in the whys and don't focus on possible solutions.

STANLEY, THE CHILD WE WEREN'T ABLE TO HELP

My first meeting with Stanley was in my university office in the mid-1960s. He came accompanied by a new set of proud and hopeful foster parents. This pair was a little on the mature side. They hovered over Stanley to be sure he said "Nice to meet you," or something to that effect to me. Stanley was all dressed up in white shirt and dark tie. His posture seemed a little rigid and he did look a little small for a five-year-old child. Because of his clothing and his bodily stance and something about his expression, he did not look much like the other boys who were in my class.

It was the hope of the people in social services that by placing Stanley in a classroom where there was a smaller adult/child ratio than in most kindergartens that he would receive necessary attention and learn how to behave better. I had been told that Stanley had been abused in his original home and as a result of this he had been taken from his birth parents and placed with foster parents. There was some mention about not getting along with children in one of the foster homes. I was given no other details about his infancy and early childhood or any therapy that he might have received.

The first day he walked into the class he looked up at the one-way screens and asked me who was behind them. I had never had a child ask about them before. I think I told him that there were people who sometimes wanted to learn about children and they came to sit in the booth and watch. I don't remember that he asked any more about it. However, I surmised from Stanley's question that he might have more fears and be more suspicions than most of the children in the class since even in his initial steps into the room he was "casing the joint."

The kindergarten lab class met in a large sunny room. There was a wide variety of activities for the children to choose from: puzzles, books, painting easel, blocks, crayons and paper, clay, house corner, etc. Stanley seemed hesitant to get involved. He often walked around from here to there and watched. One day I saw a poignant thing...Stanley was sitting on the floor next to a child who had some developmental delays. The rest of the children had already left the area at the close of a short story time. Stanley and the other child put their arms around each other's necks in a little hug with their foreheads almost touching. A few small tears were rolling down their cheeks. I think I knelt down beside them and took them by the hand and after a few minutes I helped them move on to another area. Maybe we should have explored the pain.

Early in our class sessions together, I saw Stanley becoming destructive without any observable frustration beforehand. I stayed physically close to him or I assigned one of the student teachers to shadow him. Once upon completing a routine time of juice and crackers, he swept his arm over the glasses on the table and knocked them all to the floor. Another time with no warning he picked up a chair and tried to hit another child on the head. Thankfully, the student teacher near him stopped the chair and kept a disaster from happening.

Stanley had not said he was mad or even changed the intensity in his speaking and there had been no noticeable change in his body or facial expressions before these explosions. In my past experiences I had not known or ever observed a child who did not in some way show that he was becoming frustrated or upset before he "acted out."

I consulted with a colleague who was teaching in the Psychology Dept. and he advised me that this child needed special help. "It's beyond your training," he said. "Admit it and let someone else deal with it." Indeed, our lab environment that was set up to aid and abet the development of "most" children was not meeting the needs of this child. It was sad to realize this. We did not keep Stanley in the class.

Several years later I heard that Stanley had gone through several other foster homes, but now things were going better with this last family. This new home was one that had older children who were secure and emotionally stable. Stanley "got along" with fewer problems there than he had in other situations. I do not know if he was also receiving special therapy or not.

Comments and Thoughts

Looking back now, I wonder if Stanley would have been better served by a smaller class in a smaller room with less choice time, more structure, and a psychologist/teacher that was familiar with this sort of behavior. I do think the open classroom with lots of choices and other kids working and playing might be overwhelming to some children.

The fact that the foster family with older children was able to keep Stanley and help him makes me think of the book, *Room for One More* by Anna Rose. In that true story a family with three children all agreed to work together with the mom and dad to help foster children who had severe needs. The family took in only one child at a time. Each child progressed to a state where things were generally going well before another child was added. Mrs. Rose had the ability to understand the fears and beliefs behind many of the children's behaviors. She found creative ways to help the children **change their points of view** about the world around them as well as their assumptions about themselves.

JUAN AND THE SURPRISING HAPPENINGS

Juan, a five-year-old in our Montessori school, was proficient in most classroom matters. He had come to our school when he was four. Now in the fall of his kindergarten year, he was progressing well with reading at his individual lesson. He could write numbers to 100, he enjoyed story and music times and in general was interested in all our activities. His most unusual characteristic was his consistent interest in drawing and in making up stories about his pictures.

During the two-and-a-quarter-hour activity time each day, Juan would often spend forty-five minutes to an hour at this cherished and chosen task. Other children frequently joined him at the table and watched and listened as he drew and told about his pictures. Monsters were one of his favorite themes. He drew them with skill and creativity. Everyday there was something different. And the stories continued too. Two younger boys, one three and one four who often sat with him admiringly, began to draw more and more themselves as the weeks and months went by. Soon their monsters were much more complicated than would be expected for their ages. Eventually most of the children in the class began drawing monsters and telling stories from time to time.

I found a wonderful book on mythological figures, *Eric Carle's Dragons, Dragons, and Other Creatures that Never Were*. It has colorful illustrations done with torn tissue paper. There is a name for each creature and a short poem about him or her on the same page. In the back of the book there is a glossary with more information for each creature: its country of origin, its name, and something about its importance in that country's myths and traditions. Our children were familiar with different parts of the world because of our geography program. This group of children immediately loved the book. We looked at it often and I might read about two or three different creatures each day.

Children I Have Known

I observed a burst of enthusiasm for all their art work, not just monsters. This continued throughout the year.

Comments and Thoughts

Children like Juan have taught me not to take lightly the interests and talents that they have. It is such an important vehicle for personal growth and it can be the impetus for others to grow also. I realized that it had taken months and months for this to happen…and although I always had lots of creative art happening in my classrooms, this was special and unique. I had never experienced anything quite like it and it did not ever happen like that again. It was the kind of thing a teacher can encourage, but not something that could be adult planned and programmed.

Some person once took offence at my letting these children spend so much time day after day at the same thing. One clue for me in knowing that this was good to allow and encourage was the fact that I noticed that the drawings and discussions were becoming more complicated as the weeks went by. The children were upping the ante and enjoying the challenge. In a sense, each day was not the "same thing" at all.

In succeeding years, I tried to use the book about the mythological creatures but the children did not seem very interested. I think this is a good example of how building interest and skills over many months lays the foundation for learning more. **Without the foundation, the "more" is not very interesting. With a foundation many things are possible.**

Another example of this principle occurred as follows. As a part of my volunteer work after retirement I went once a week for about a half-hour story session in a kindergarten class at Dry Creek Elementary School. This particular year the author Patricia Polacco had come to visit this school. In preparation, all the children had learned about her life and had been introduced to many of the books that she had written and illustrated. There was great enthusiasm for her visit and she connected readily with the children.

At Easter time I brought Polacco's book *Rechenka's Eggs* to read. The children recognized it was one of "her" books when I took it from the basket in preparation for reading. Several children offered to tell me about Patricia Polacco's life or something that happened when she had come to visit. This class eagerly listened and watched as I read. There was a joy and synergy that day that was noticeably beyond what had happened in previous years when I read that book to other groups of children.

I guess I have felt for years that there must always be a good program in every class, basic skills need to be learned, every child needs to progress in each area of study, but hopefully there is room for "the surprising" to happen now and then. If we make room for it by allowing and nurturing **in-depth, connected, and ongoing experiences** for children then "a good surprise" is more likely to happen. And when it does, it will feed our souls in another dimension.

BARBARA, THE CASE OF THE "DETERMINED" CHILD

Barbara arrived at preschool as a very determined four-year-old. I remember the first time she came to the line to wait her turn to go wash. She came around other children to the front of the line. I informed her that the proper thing was for each child to go to the back of the line and wait his or her turn. She looked at me and refused to budge. I said nothing more to her. I called the name of the child who had been first and simply had her walk around Barbara. Then I called the name of each child in succession and had them go in turn and finally I told Barbara she could go.

In the future, she went to the end of the line, but she never looked very pleased about it. As weeks and months went by, I observed that this child showed a wide variety of emotions and expressed her positive and her negative feelings well. In her play and work she was lively and actively engaged. She concentrated on her activities. She was a fast learner. In her social activities, there were times when she was upset when the person she wanted to play with was busy doing something else or when things didn't work out as she planned.

About three months later I noticed a great deal of compliance on the part of this child and what seemed to me to be an overly active interest in pleasing adults and other children. At the same time I was observing a diminished determination in her work and less intense interest in carrying out her own ideas.

I became concerned for this child. I spoke with her parents about what I was observing and asked them to observe any changes at home. I encouraged honesty of feeling at appropriate times and not expecting the child to be happy all the time. Within several weeks Barbara had returned to her old full-of-spirit personality.

Comments and Thoughts

I had recently heard a speech by Mary Pipher and I also had read her book, *Reviving Ophelia*. The ideas in the speech and book rekindled many of my own thoughts and gave me the necessary push I needed to focus on the recent changes I had seen in Barbara and to discuss them with her parents.

It is interesting to think about our lifelong need to balance our own interests and the development of our talents and abilities with the need to get along with others. Piper's book speaks to the special problems of adolescent girls as they face the influences of peers and the general culture that pushes them to set aside their unique, active, and often bold interests to become sweet, passive, and "more ladylike." I am wondering if in some cases many girls face those often damaging "expectations" even as young children.

JANE AND THE GOOD RESULTS OF "BAD BEHAVIOR"

Jane was a four-year-old girl in one of my university lab school classes. She could not control all her muscles in a normal way and her gait was halting. Her speech seemed slightly affected and her disabilities made her appear a little "different." I did not know any details of her infancy or what help or therapy she and the family had received in the past. She seemed to play and enjoy the activities much like the other children her age. I did notice that some of the girls seemed to shy away from being near her. Anyway, I tried my best as the teacher to treat her as I would have any other child. Down deep, I probably felt sorry for her.

One day at rest time after the children were all lying down on their cots, Jane picked up the broom from the housekeeping play area, and stuck it out in front of me as I walked by her cot.

Needless to say I was quite upset as I almost stumbled over the broom. In that moment I forgot all about Jane's birth defects and just explained in no uncertain terms that what she had done was a terribly dangerous thing to do. She cracked a little smile. I thought that meant she did it on purpose as a joke or something.

Well, from that moment on I did not feel sorry for Jane. Somehow the spontaneous misbehavior and chastisement had leveled the playing field for all of us. She began to get along better with all the children and the assistants and with me. I began to observe her quick mind and her personality now and I paid little attention to her "problems."

Comments and Thoughts

I learned from Jane the great value sometimes of "bad behavior." This child suddenly became totally normal to me. Maybe Jane was in some way trying, albeit unconsciously, to do something that would upset and change the dynamics of what had been happening in that classroom. At some level she must have felt my "sympathy" toward her and possibly some wariness and avoidance from the other children. Those were my assumptions at the time.

In retrospect it occurs to me that possibly her play was rougher than that of the other little girls and that maybe that was the reason they shied away initially from playing with her rather than some fear connected with her looks or "disabilities." I believe she had two older brothers she frequently played with in a rough and tumble way. Maybe teasing was also a part of their play.

I read one time that we should try to think of three possible reasons why anyone behaves a certain way...that helps us to be more open-minded and less likely to base our actions on faulty interpretations.

LINDA AND IMPROVING COMMUNICATION

I had attended a demonstration workshop in Missoula in which we were shown how to use the beginning communication exercises explained in a series of books, *Methods in Human Development* by **Bessell and Palomares**. I arrived at home that afternoon, all excited about improving communication with children. As we worked on the supper I told our children, Linda, Cliff, Lucky, and Janet, a little about this program and how interesting it was. Then we sat down to eat. During the meal I suggested that we could play the game of the "magic box" right now. "We have this lovely pretend magic box right in the middle of our table," I explained to the children, "and there is something in it that would make you happy." Each child and I thought for a moment and then we went around the table and told the others something that would make us happy. I was sorry my husband was out of town working and missing all this fun! Everyone participated and I thought, wow, even older kids think this is great!

After supper, Linda's cat was missing so she went out to try to find him. About an hour or so later she came back in the house. She was tired, but happy that she had found her cat. Then she looked into the kitchen and saw all the supper dishes still piled up, her job to do. She looked at me and said, "Oh, Mother, I thought you would have known...my highest joy...would have been for you to have done the dishes!"

Comments and Thoughts

I thought how interesting that Linda integrated the ideas we had discussed with her own feelings of the moment and communicated all that in such a poignant and humorous way. It certainly gave me increased awareness of her bright and quick mind. She was in general a quiet child who did not express to me many of her inner thoughts. Later, I thought to myself...how embarrassing that I never thought about those dishes.

After that experience, I realized that many times knowing more about what someone thinks or feels increases the complexity of things and it is not always comfortable. It often does not solve the immediate problem (re: the dishes), but it may affect our underlying assumptions about what other people think or need and hopefully it may improve communication in ways that benefit the relationship in the long run.

I never used the complete program described in detail in the Bessell/Palomares book series, *Methods in Human Development*. I did use some of the beginning "magic circle" activities at various times with each class of children that I had from that time on. These were the exercises I had seen demonstrated at the workshop. I found children enjoyed the activity and it increased our understanding of each other. The name "magic circle" I do not find readily as I look back through the book series that I have at hand. Maybe there was another name for the activity originally.

Another session with the "magic circle" that I well remember was with a group of three-year-olds. After all the children had told what would make them happy, I asked the children what they thought would make me happy. Someone suggested a play helicopter. Someone said candy. Typically we think others want what we would like. As I shook my head each time, the children looked quite puzzled. Finally one little girl looked up and said, "Oh, I know," and then she smiled broadly and added, "A little baby." I smiled back, nodded in agreement, and wiped away a small tear.

My abbreviated use of this program reminds me of what often happens with workshop participants. We take home one good idea and try to make use of it. Maybe that is a realistic outcome. I did buy the whole series of books. They looked interesting and I read a little and glanced at all of them. I believe that to have done a thorough job using the complete program I should have completed an extended class with study and practice. And even then I would have had to give up something in my preschool program to make room for these activities. It might have been worth it.

As a provider of workshop programs in recent years, I often missed the cue on what and how to teach in a short session. Sometimes I have tried to give a huge amount of "good information." It is probably a mistake to try to cram into a small amount of time, material which needs to be processed in a long period of study replete with opportunity to reflect, practice, and question.

PETE AND THE PERPLEXING VERBAL CONTRARINESS

This child came to my class preschool and kindergarten one fall because he was having trouble adapting to a regular kindergarten class. A friend of his mother's was familiar with our school and she suggested it as a possibility to Pete's mother. I was glad we had room in our multi-age class and that the other ten children in my room were fairly "squared away" and not presenting any major problems.

Pete would say things like, "Who are you to tell me what to do?", "I'm not doing that," or "Don't count on me," etc., etc. I had never had a child with this same sort of verbal contrariness in my previous classes. However, I did not sense any underlying "hostility." There was never any physical aggression. The other children seemed puzzled at his language just as I was. Fortunately the rest of the class tried joining me in my philosophical attitude of trying to figure out how we could all get along better.

I looked for a place in our day that seemed to go well. It was the individual lesson time where I had ten minutes a day teaching each child. Peter enjoyed this work session and made rapid progress. He had a phenomenal memory. He learned to read so quickly that we were all amazed. The other children would say things like, "How can this be?" I would smile and reassure them that they were progressing fine and that Pete was especially talented in learning to read and we all have areas that are easier or harder for us.

The difficult verbal interaction, at other times during our day, still continued. I sought help in how to deal with this. I went to a presentation at Peninsula College about children who have a certain type of disorder which I thought this child might have. After hearing the presentation, I doubted that this was my child's difficulty. I went to the Internet and looked for further information on the topic. I read a lot. At the end of one of the papers on the Internet, someone suggested other topics to look up. I clicked onto one of the other subjects. Within minutes I had before me a list of characteristics many of which were similar to those of my child. I was amazed. There was also a list of practical suggestions for parents and teachers.

I shared some of the information I found with the family and suggested that they might want to have their son tested in order to find out more. We studied the list of practical things that parents and teachers could try. One idea was to keep a little book in which the teacher could write down significant things and the child could take it home each day. Likewise the parents could write and the teacher could read each morning. The parents and I both kept the little book going. Writing the observations gave us new insights. It also gave us something to do rather than focusing only on the contrary language at that moment. And we did not have to depend on our memory for how often certain behaviors occurred. One thing I noticed was that there did not seem to be much correlation between home and school in the sense that Pete could have a great morning at home and then arrive at school and have many difficult interactions. Or just the opposite could have happened: a calm day at school after a difficult morning at home.

Eventually, when something negative began happening between us, Pete would see me getting out the book to write. He might then change his attitude and say something to the effect, "Well, let's start again. Maybe I can explain what I meant in a different way."

Another technique worked well with Pete. It was giving short instructions to have him change a physical position before discussing any problem. Whenever I saw him doing something that he wasn't supposed to do, I did not tell him to stop. Instead I'd say, "Pete, please sit down. Thank you, Pete." Then I would discuss what the problem was or what I wanted him to do, etc. He seemed somewhat able to cope with the situation without verbal hostility toward me when I used this method.

After he learned to read well, it occurred to me to try giving him written messages rather than oral. It was amazing. Pete reacted totally differently than he had to my verbal suggestions and corrections. He seemed to like reading and figuring out the message and proving to me that he understood by following my instructions!

Comments

I learned many things from working with Pete. My basic belief that some children can be helped with methods not commonly used in the classroom was again proved true.

I was careful in talking with the family not to make guesses as to what the "problem" was. I had learned in graduate school that the diagnosis of children's disorders should be left to a specialist in that field of psychology or medicine. I shared my "observations" of this child with the family. I did counsel the family to seek professional help in order to learn more and to be able to help Pete as effectively as possible.

Often a professional diagnosis and plan of action can greatly help everyone in efforts to work successfully with a child. Putting the child's problems in proper context and seeing the total child, not just the "problems," should be a valuable component of the work with the doctor or psychologist.

One other thought about this particular child, Pete. I believe the fact that he learned to read so successfully gave him a feeling of some accomplishment and importance. When he went to first grade the next year he was reading at a second-grade level or beyond. We all need areas of competence. And when the area of competence is vital to learning other things then the gain is multiplied many times over for the child. We also need to see ourselves as people who have the capacity to learn. Pete's ability to read probably helped his concept of seeing himself as a child who can learn and who likes to learn. But of course one competency does not make up for everything.

Pete's social skills did improve a little during the year. Did learning to read help Pete's interaction with other children? It seemed to me that maybe it did in a roundabout way. I have noticed that children often want to play with children whose abilities they admire. Frequently that may be the impetus to get acquainted. Once a child is interacting with another child, it may take other things to aid and abet the relationship, but without something to help start it, it might not happen at all.

JASON, AND THE PROBLEM WITH "B" AND "D"

Jason came to our Montessori school class when he was four. He got along well with the other children and he enjoyed a wide variety of activities like puzzles, drawing, games, story time, etc. He came readily to have his individual lesson with me. He learned his numbers 1 to 9 in about average time for a child his age using our tactile numbers and teaching with the "Three Period Lesson." (See discussion in Part VI for information on this method of instruction.) Initially he might write a number or two backwards, but he recognized each one and knew what quantity it stood for. Within several months he usually made his numbers correctly. He seemed to love his number work and by spring he and his best friend would each get a paper with one hundred squares and spend twenty to thirty minutes writing numbers almost every day. I would often look up and see the boys smiling and chatting now and then as they worked.

When Jason began to learn the sounds with the tactile letters, he had no trouble learning "b." It was probably one of the first ten letter sounds he learned. It was when I introduced him to "d," many sounds later, the confusion began. I backed up in his individual lessons. I reviewed the "b." We traced the tactile "b" with our fingers. We said, "bu,bu,bu" baseball bat. "Look, here is the bat and here is the ball in front of it." This did not work for Jason. In his mind he understood no difference between the "b" and the "d."

So what to do? He knew his colors. So I made a special "b" card that showed a black regular "b" covered with blue transparent accent marker. He practiced "b" for blue and took his fingers and went over the letter just as we did earlier with the felt letters.

He learned all his other letter sounds and was ready to start learning short three-letter phonetic words. Each day, we reviewed the "b" sound with the blue marker over the black letter. Then we began to sound out words. I asked Jason to pause when he came to a "b" or "d." Before saying the sound he checked to see if the letter in the word on the card was going the same way as the letter with the blue accent left on the table near him. Although he could not get it right if just left to his memory, he could tell that it was going in the same direction if he compared the letter visually to his known "b" with the blue accent. I had him check each time he saw a "b" or a "d" before he made the sound so he would make the correct sound. I felt he was compounding his confusion if he voiced the wrong sound for either letter.

This system helped him. He got quicker and quicker at making his reference check. Often when seeing the word in the book and understanding the context he knew it. If he hesitated I had a blue-tipped pointer that I would put under the "b" and that was his cue. I did not have to interrupt his speaking or thought processes with any sound from me. The pointer was a piece of wooden dowel about the diameter of a pencil and about six inches long, which had been sharpened in a pencil sharpener. In this case I had painted the point blue.

Jason was at our school for two years, his four-year-old year and for kindergarten. He was reading well at the end of his kindergarten year. I saw his mother once during his first-grade year and she was thrilled with his progress. "Hey, this kid rushes every day for the newspaper to read the comics!"

Comments

This was another example of how important it is to find some way of teaching a child that works for that child. The left/right direction of the shape of a letter evidently was confused in this child's brain…color was clear to him. We probably all learn better when there is a connection to something we are not confused about. I had to find a connection that would be understandable to him in order to make the initial learning possible. And then somehow his brain took over and could read without the "connection."

We are learning a lot about the brain today and we are aware that not all children learn best in the same way. Just because a child does not grasp something initially as it is presented to a group, or even individually, does not mean he can not learn it if it is presented differently. Thankfully most schools have extra help available now for the child who needs it. Parents may get materials to use for helping the child at home either from the school or library. If the child does not make progress, hiring a private tutor may be a good investment.

I had a friend many years ago whose first grader was not progressing in reading. She knew her other children had learned okay at that age. She found the explanation from the teacher of "Don't worry about it...he'll catch on later," not very satisfactory. She searched for help and found a special clinic for children who were having trouble learning. The clinic worked with her child for about six months and the child began to read. The clinic teacher told this child that he could accomplish anything his friends could…it would just take him three times longer. Most things in school did take him longer, but he persevered and even learned to enjoy studying.

Sudie Doughton Mason

ETHAN AND THE MYSTERY IN THE BATHROOM

Ethan came to my class for his "before kindergarten" year. He was a cheerful child and he was interested in a wide range of activities. I remember a wonderful collage of animal pictures the class cut out and pasted together as a result of one of Ethan's many interests. He seemed in every way to be a competent and "full of vitality" four-year-old.

I had a multi-age group of twelve children with a small three-year-old boy as the youngest. Probably it was in late October or early November that the janitor noticed urine on the floor in the boys' bathroom. The first several times it happened, the janitor cleaned it up. Eventually his patience ran out, and I could see he was getting pretty exasperated about this. I certainly was getting tired of it too. I had discussed it with the boys and reminded them to be careful, etc. So this day when he came by my door and motioned to me, I followed him into the bathroom to inspect the problem. I reacted with consternation and the determination that today we would get to the bottom of this.

I returned to the room and told all the boys to line up and come see the "problem." The youngest boy was not there that day…and in the back of my mind I had assumed it was he who was the cause of this trouble. I felt certain now that my assumption had been wrong. All the boys looked at the mess on the floor near one of the toilets. One by one I looked them in the eye and asked, "Did you do this?" Finally Ethan broke down and cried and said it was his fault and he would clean it up. The other children were dismissed back to the room with a parent who was helping that day. I stayed with Ethan and we worked on the floor together. Finally we were done. Ethan straightened up and we went back in the classroom and back to work.

About ten minutes later Ethan came over to my table and looked at me and said, "Sudie, you did not ask me why I did it."

I stared at him a moment in surprise and then said, "Oh, okay, why did you do it?"

"Well, it was like this," he said, "Johnny told me there was a monster down in the toilet and I'd better not get too close!" I was taken aback a bit, but I looked a little quizzically at him in case he had more to add. He kind of looked back at me with a quizzical look of his own as if to say, so what would you have expected me to do? I gave him a nod of understanding. "Well, it must not be so," he added. He smiled and went back to his work.

Comments

Ethan had developed the ability to speak to the adult and he had the confidence to explain his point of view to me. He also had the common sense to wait until I had calmed down and the mess cleaned up before he said anything to me about his reasons.

The child who had done the teasing was there and overheard everything. He seemed quiet and thoughtful. I did not call him over to discuss the matter. He was in general a competent and caring child just as Ethan was. I think there are times when maybe the less said the better. This is an important call for the teacher to make.

This was another situation that was caused by something totally outside my ideas about what the problem might be. I had always tried to emphasize real and imaginary with the children and to talk with them about those concepts at story time. I made a special effort to do that now. Also at times we talked in general about teasing.

In my childhood, when I had told on my brother for teasing me and as a result my parents had called him in for specific discussion about what he had said and done, it seemed like he did not want to play with me after that. Later, I had a good friend who had told me that a black cat came out of her black onyx ring at night. I thought it was a little frightening but I did not tell my mother, because I did not want her to interfere in our friendship.

In this situation, thankfully, the boys' friendship did not seem to be negatively affected and they played and worked together frequently. Other ways of handling this might have worked or been important to use with other children. It would be a good topic for parents and teachers to discuss.

Certainly our own childhood experiences influence how we feel about certain types of "happenings" with children. We need to become consciously aware of this and not let our own immediate feelings or reactions be the only thing that we go by in deciding how to deal with a situation.

Sudie Doughton Mason

JEFF AND THE DAILY SHORT TUTORING SESSION

Jeff was an eight-year-old in the third grade when I met him. His mother had heard from a friend that I was tutoring children in the afternoons. She called to see if I thought I could help her child. It seemed that Jeff was not catching up in reading even though both the school and the family had tried to help him. Jeff's mother brought him by for an initial interview with me. I realized that this child would need a lot of help.

I told the mother that I believed Jeff would profit most from coming to me every afternoon after school for about thirty minutes for each session. This was a lot of transportation on her part but she was willing to do it. Jeff and I worked at a table in my office. He seemed interested in everything in the house and he was quite a charming child. He often tried to engage me in conversation about the rock collection or the dog or anything other than our "work."

I felt a good rapport with this child immediately. But teaching and learning were not easy. His reading skills were so poor that I decided to back up all the way and go through the complete way of teaching reading that Betty and I had used in our school. Jeff was often fidgety and seemed to glance from here to there rather than concentrating on the lesson.

In my storeroom of "helpful activities and equipment," I had the **balance board invented by Dr. Frank Belgau** whose youngest child had been a student in our Montessori school. This special piece of equipment was a board on top of little rockers. Its purpose was to help the child focus and gain balance and control. The child stood on it with feet aligned a certain way and by concentrating he could keep his balance. This activity could be made more difficult by having the child put a beanbag on his head or catch one while he was on the balance board. It could also be made more difficult by changing the angle of the rockers. For more information about Dr. Belgau and his work, go to his **web site Balametrics**. (I have received permission to mention this in this book.)

I had used this board successfully over the years in my Montessori class with children who needed something to help them focus before beginning an individual reading lesson. I introduced the board to Jeff early in our acquaintance and he liked it and it helped him "get himself together" and to be able to concentrate on his reading. It was not always necessary to use it. Some days Jeff was calm and focused.

Jeff already knew many of the phonetic sounds for the letters. Soon he had mastered them all and we were making short, three-letter phonetic words with short vowel sounds. Then we went through all the long vowel sounds, slowly and carefully. The beginning books were relatively easy and went well for Jeff, but eventually things got longer and harder. Some days he would kind of just put his head down at a funny angle and not try. I had never had a child who had gotten through the beginning phonetic books and had so much trouble with the continuing ones in the series.

I tried discussing the situation and got nowhere. Backing up to easier material worked, but the minute we started with slightly longer and harder things, the problem reoccurred. What to do? Suddenly the words *skookum* and *tumtum* came to my mind. In the old Chinook jargon, skookum meant strong; *tumtum* meant heart, mind, and will (Charles Lillard, A *Great Voice Within Us,* p. 82). The words seemed to express vibrantly what Jeff needed. So I told him about Chinook, a wonderful kind of language that made it possible for the many varied "First Nations" tribes of the Coastal Northwest and the early explorers and later settlers to understand each other. I told him I knew he had a strong heart and mind and that to remind him when I thought he needed to use it I would whisper the words, "*skookum tumtum.*" At the same time I would beat with my fist gently on my chest. These words and this little motion to my heart somehow made a connection with this child.

From then on when I saw him first begin to lag or not keep good posture during his lesson, I would make a little beat on my chest and whisper, "*skookum tumtum.*" Jeff would immediately sit up straighter and begin to try. Soon no words were necessary, just the soft beat of my fist on my chest. It was like a game between us. His ability to continue even when it got hard increased dramatically.

Another thing that helped Jeff was having him read loudly and distinctly. He tended to drop the volume on the final sounds of the words. I would leave the room and challenge him to read loud enough so that I could hear every sound in each word and I would go farther and farther from where he was. This intrigued him and he accepted the challenge. Maybe my not being in eyesight of the child reduced the distraction that my own presence might have been. The situation was also a little ridiculous and fun, which Jeff related to with glee.

Jeff came to me the next year also, but we reduced the sessions to four afternoons a week. We read harder and harder materials and we would discuss the reading afterwards. He had a terrible time reading material in a dialect. But an interesting thing happened with that too. His school put on a play and he had to memorize his lines in a kind of southern dialect. Lo and behold, after that he did not have so much trouble reading stories that included conversations in dialect.

Comments

Jeff was a good example of a child that could learn with sufficient help. In this case, as with most children with learning problems, I think it was important that I observed the child carefully at all times. I had to use the information about him I was learning from observing and working with him and then I had to sift through my experiences of the past and to some extent use my own imagination as to how best to proceed. I think when Jeff first came to me, he already thought that he could not learn like other children. Maybe that assessment at that time was reality and in some ways he was smart to know that. Betty and other teachers had told me that often children who are the most behind don't realize it themselves. So I guessed that this kid was potentially capable.

This child had a lot of support to help him continue to make progress once he got on a **learning track**. His family was helpful in everyway possible. He was involved in community activities and also had grandparents who were interested in his welfare. After his beginning years in public school, his parents placed him in a private school where there were fewer children in each class room. Several years ago he started music lessons. At present he is back in public school and making mostly A's and a few B's!

Many times there are programs for children who are behind, but they are not sufficient in intensity, in finding exactly what is needed to help the child progress, and in daily practice where both the adult and the child recognize what is being learned and **as a natural consequence feel successful.**

I believe that after-school tutoring with a child for a short period each day is more conducive to progress than working three times a week for an hour each time. This might not be true for older children or children with a less pronounced problem. I am not aware of research on this but it would be a very interesting subject to study. One of the problems with the once a week or three times a week scenario is that if the child is absent for some reason then the amount of time between sessions is greatly extended. The resulting losses are often compounded.

One further comment, this time about how children sometimes relate well to special motions or words to get their attention and help them control their own behavior. I remember reading years ago about a woman who was trying to help her new stepchild overcome some strange mannerisms. She found that conversations with him about it made matters worse, so she developed a little secret code of hand motions that she would show the child in such a way that no one else could see. The child would immediately become aware of his behavior and he would make an effort to improve.

Another time I remember a teacher shared with me that she had success teaching young children to follow certain instructions by teaching them the commands in Spanish, e.g., *anda muy lento* "walk slowly," *anda mas rapido* "walk faster," *sientese por favor* "sit, please," etc. I tried it and found it very successful also. The children just loved hearing and understanding words in another language and seemed very proud that they could so easily follow those instructions!

POLLY AND THE CHILDREN FACE A WAR

Polly was a delightful five-year-old child in one of my Montessori classes. She got along well with the other children and she seemed to enjoy most of the school activities. She especially liked creative art work and stories. She would draw and cut out figures and even make three-dimensional things like a baby carriage with a baby inside. Some days she spent forty-five minutes to an hour on her creations. For show-and-tell she would bring up what she had made and she would tell the children a short story using her characters and props. Her ability to keep the attention of the other children was an unusual accomplishment for a five-year-old.

She stayed so busy concentrating on her activities that often she would be the last child for the individual lesson. As a rule I did not interrupt a child who was concentrating on a project, but everyone had to have a little lesson each day so after finishing with other students, she would be called to come. It became like a little game with us and she would look up and see me smile and motion to her and she would quickly put her things in her locker and come and sit beside me for her lesson. I'm not sure what all this has to do with the main subject of "the war," but one of my friends advised me to tell more about the children, not just things about the main topic.

When the first war with Saddam Hussein broke out, my children arrived at the afternoon class quite upset. The boys were saying things like, "We'll show them!" "Let's go after them," etc. The girls didn't seem to be saying much, but they seemed pensive. I suggested we have a circle time right now and discuss the situation and what we were thinking. Usually we waited until later in the day for circle time. The children sat down and one by one they began to say again some of the things they had said when they entered the room. Somebody asked why stuff like this happens and one older boy answered, "Well, didn't you guys know adults have their problems too?" There were more comments and finally Polly said, "I think we should pray about this."

I suggested that she could lead the prayer. Polly instructed the children to hold hands and get ready to pray. Then she said something to the effect, "Lord, please keep all the children in the world safe. We don't want anyone to die."

Comments

I was surprised at the intense reactions of the children. They had probably been at home in the morning with adults who were watching it all on TV and making comments. Yet I was still shocked and it gave me cause to wonder about the strong difference in reaction among the boys and the girls. However, not one single boy declined to join Polly and the rest of us in prayer.

I learned from this that unusual happenings can give us a

window into children's feelings and interpretations of things. Also an out-of-the-routine occurrence or crisis may give a child an opportunity to lead in a way we normally would not have available.

I believe Polly had lost an older brother in a car accident. Her personal experience with tragedy may be one of the reasons she was so concerned and took the leadership in this situation. I have learned from Polly and many other children that if you provide an atmosphere that allows children to take initiative and encourages them to do so, they frequently will.

I felt taking the few minutes to discuss the children's thoughts about this situation was a way of respecting their concerns and acknowledging the seriousness of war. I also knew that it would probably be impossible for the children to really concentrate on their work without first coping with their feelings about this crisis. The fact that a certain level of trust existed between the children and me was another factor in their openness and sharing.

DAVE, A RECEPTIVE AND EXPRESSIVE CHILD

Dave was a gregarious and active child. He seemed to take in everything that was going on and he progressed well and with ease in all our areas of study. During the November that Dave was five, we had several stories and books about various Native American groups that populated North America in the 1600s. We also had books about the first Thanksgiving. Dave's mother brought a copy of a *Weekly Reader's* special edition (for primary age children) about the Mayflower, the Puritans, the Native Americans, and what the first Thanksgiving was like. All the children in our school were interested in the details of the clothing, food stuffs, what the kids were doing, the kind of little boats at that time, etc.

All of their interest inspired me to try to explain to the children how Bill, my husband, was a descendent of the people who came on the Mayflower. Now of course I knew that five-year-olds and younger children don't always understand time concepts, but I proceeded anyway.

I reminded the children of the stories we had studied about the Mayflower and Thanksgiving. Then I said, "Well, one of the couples on the Mayflower was Robert and Susanna White and they had two little boys. The older boy, Resolved, was about five years old when they came across on the ship. He was the age many of you are now! Eventually the years passed and Resolved grew up and married a woman whose name was Judith Vassall. Resolved and Judith had a child, Elizabeth, who grew up and married Obadiah Wheeler. He grew up and married and had a child named Jonathan."

I had all the names, generation by generation, on a large chart; I read the names and proceeded with the story. The children seemed wide-eyed and fascinated. I came to the end of the list and continued, "Helen Wheeler married Lloyd Mason, and their first child was a little boy, Bill. He grew up and married me! You know that man who comes by in the blue truck to pick up the tuition checks? Well, that's Bill, my husband. His great-great-great-great-great-great-great-great-grandparents came over on the Mayflower!"

A couple of days later my husband came by in the blue truck and stopped in the alley behind the school room. I opened a window to hand him the checks. Soon I overheard Dave in the adjoining room say to another boy, "See that guy in the blue pick-up...he's the one that came over on the Mayflower!" I chuckled to myself as I realized that Dave was making sense of my presentation as best he could.

Another Dave story occurred many months later one Friday before Mother's Day. We had completed making our stationery for our mothers by screen-spatter painting. We had wrapped the gifts and the children would take them home that day. Many of the mothers were waiting in the hall for school to be over.

We were just finishing up our music time with the song, "You Are My Sunshine." Dave looked up and with a big smile said, "Let's sing 'You Are My Mother'." I smiled and nodded agreement. I opened the door so the mothers and fathers could come in and all the children sang, "You are my mother, my only mother, you make me happy when skies are grey, you'll never know, dear, how much I love you, please don't take my mother away."

I'm sure there was a smile on my face and tears in my eyes that day as I joined the children in singing about love for our mothers.

Children I Have Known

We sang Dave's version every year after that...for the mothers on Mother's Day.

Comments

In the earlier story about the Mayflower, I have wondered if it would have been more understandable to the children if I had used puppets or cut out figures to tell the story. With more concrete things to look at and a better explanation of the passage of time, maybe the story would have made more sense. Yet in retrospect I have always thought Dave was right. Bill retains so many of the old Puritan virtues such as seriousness and hard work; he is like one of them! I smile to myself and wonder...do children sometimes know our underlying thoughts?

I think the important concept for parents and teachers to remember is that children see and hear many things that are not understandable to them in the way they are to adults. We may connect with the child in some way no matter what we are discussing, but the child will not necessarily pick up the information exactly as we ourselves think we are saying it and explaining it. And although it may appear funny or strange to us, we must never laugh at a child because of this. Any important information needs to be discussed from time to time as a child is growing older so that the child's maturing mentality and experiences are brought to bear on the subject matter. It is important to get feedback from the child and not assume what he/she knows and understands. It is also important to try to see things through a child's eyes.

There are many times that children do not necessarily "take in" what the adult thought they were explaining. The following story came from a family I knew from my teaching in a parent co-op. The father was a policeman and he and the mother had gone to great lengths explaining to their little girl about what her father did every day and how many people he helped, etc. But one day after all their efforts, a new neighborhood child came to visit. The mother overheard her child explain to her new friend, "Hey, my dad's a policeman — and he shoots people!"

The child probably remembered what her parents had said and she had integrated that with what she already had learned by watching TV and hearing children talk. In this instance she

Sudie Doughton Mason

just said what she probably thought was the most important and powerful comment she could make!

Part II
Subjects Dear to My Heart

In memory of my father,   **George Edward Doughton, Sr.**

    Papa always took time for us kids. He had rocked me at night for six months when I was an infant with colic. When we were little he took us places and explained things. He never seemed to be in a hurry like most people. He made us wooden clogs one summer. He made us a great sled one winter and took us sledding in the moonlight when it was finished. Papa played the days and seasons as they came. He liked to talk and to listen. He always saw three or four sides to most things. He had a good sense of humor and told lots of stories from his own life. He helped to extend our frame of reference. In my teens, he would help with homework, take you where you needed to go, and give you advice about how to act when you got there. He questioned me about my thoughts and ideas and he shared his opinions if he thought he should. Papa seemed "present" in each moment.

    "Try to get the lay of land." That was one of my dad's favorite sayings. I have always remembered that. He warned me that talking too much would interfere with my getting an "in depth" and realistic picture of what was going on around me.

"It's got to be simple" was another saying he would use when he would set about to fix a broken refrigerator or help with a math problem. "We got here, honey, we can figure out how to get out,"…he would say if we were lost on a road somewhere. Other statements I remember are, "Don't panic." "There is more than one way to figure this out." "You can learn from any subject you study." "Everything doesn't turn out the way you think it is going to." "Most people have far more brain power than they use."

Honor was important to him. Confidence was important. He knew some things were more valuable than others and that some things required sacrifice. He was not averse to taking a chance if one had assessed the risk.

Papa remembered the past, lived in the present, and he thought about the future and the children who would be born someday. Just as he had enjoyed his children and grandchildren, he would have been thrilled with all the "great-grandchildren" coming along now.

There was a story about Papa when he was a little boy, the youngest of five children. He came down the steps one morning and into the kitchen where his mother was and he showed her how he could snap his fingers. As she watched in appreciation of the new skill, he commented, "Look what I have learned to do, and I didn't even have to have a book!"

In the years while I was growing up, I never saw Papa spend much time with books. I asked him once about that and he commented that he had read a lot when he was younger and it seemed to him that so many times books just repeated each other or something to that effect. He liked to spend his time with his family, or inventing, making, or fixing things. He loved traveling about and adventuring. I can't think about him without smiling. He seemed alive and aware in ways that few people are. There was no one best certain road to walk down. Although, he would have thought some roads were much better than others! I don't think he put a lot of stock in books, but it probably would have been okay with him for me to write one, as long as I didn't take it all too seriously!

Foreword

Over the years I have written many little editorials, outlines, and other general short papers usually for college students or for participants at workshops. When my oldest three grandchildren, Paul, Lisa, and Tammy, first became parents I often wanted to share ideas with them, but we lived so far apart that I could not keep up with the happenings of their families. Writing down my experiences, ideas, etc. in the form of a book which they could refer to from time to time seemed a good plan. So that is one of my reasons for writing this section of the book! I have grouped the material in Part II in three sections: "Especially for Parents," "For Parents and Teachers," and "Especially for Teachers."

I would also like to add a word of appreciation for **Paul, Lisa, Tammy, and Christopher**, the grandchildren from Montana who went boating with us up into British Columbia waters in the 1980s and in the 1990s. Our summer experiences together meant an in-depth opportunity for us get to know each child in many specials ways. And what fun it was seeing the wonders of nature through their eyes!

Christopher, the youngest of those four, has the excitement and challenge of marriage and parenthood still ahead of him; likewise so do **Bradley and Amanda**, grandchildren who live in Tennessee.

I want to remind the readers that this book is my interpretation of the subject matter. **It is not the final word about anything.** It may seem "old and out of date"...which of course it is in some ways. However, many of the ideas that I came to appreciate most in the later years of my work were from educational materials developed more than fifty years before I discovered them. In our continual search for how to successfully work with and teach children, reviewing old methods that worked well may be as important as discovering new methods.

ESPECIALLY FOR PARENTS

BUILDING A GOOD PARENT/CHILD RELATIONSHIP

LIKE YOURSELF. Accept yourself and be true to your best self. Remember if you don't like yourself, it is hard to like someone else and your children may find it hard to like you. Follow some of your own interests. Continue to grow and become the person you want to be.

BE DEPENDABLE.

LEARN ABOUT YOUR CHILDREN. Talk and discuss things with your children. Find out their opinions and ideas. Keep observing and learning about your children. Observe them at play...the games and toys they like, the people they like to play with, etc. Observe them with pets. Observe them at meal time...what foods they especially like or dislike, etc. Observe what things are easy or hard for them. Try to become aware of each child's own inner rhythms.

HELP YOUR CHILDREN KNOW MORE ABOUT YOU. Let the children know your opinions and some of the things that make you happy and sad. Share pictures and stories from your childhood that they can relate to and understand. As the children get older, you can point out situations in your own life, what options you had available to choose from, and what happened as a result of your choices. A short commentary on these things at appropriate moments may be better than drawn-out discussions.

HELP EACH CHILD DEVELOP TALENTS AND INTERESTS. First look for and notice the talents and interests of your child. Don't expect your child to have the same talents and interests that you had. Do not expect your child to be equally successful and interested in all things. Respect the child's endeavors. Try not to interrupt him when he is working hard on something. As the child grows and has new experiences, new talents and interests may become evident.

SPEND SPECIAL TIME WITH EACH CHILD EACH DAY. It might only be five or ten minutes but it provides an opportunity for you to focus especially on each child as an individual.

PROVIDE OPPORTUNITIES FOR YOUR CHILD TO HAVE FRIENDS OF MANY AGES.
Other adults and children outside the family can frequently offer new and different ways of looking at life to a child. A neighbor, a Sunday school teacher, a piano teacher, an uncle or aunt, etc. may appreciate and enjoy your child and mentor your child in important ways. A friendship with another child may be fostered by the two children having time to play together without the competition from others.

GIVE CHEERFULLY. When you give to your young children, do so with an open heart and cheerfully. If something is not good for them or must be withheld for some reason, simply say no in a matter-of-fact way or explain further if that seems to help. Have confidence in your judgment calls. Do not lament and groan and then give in.

MAINTAIN YOUR AUTHORITY. Remember you are in charge. Do not abdicate that responsibility. The child will feel overburdened with decisions and fears and with more than he can handle. Being "in charge" with children does not mean you don't love them. To the contrary, there are times when your firmness, combined with love and interest in what is best for the child, may contribute greatly to a happy life even if the child is not so happy every moment.

HAVE A GOOD DAILY AND WEEKLY ROUTINE. Meals served on time and a time to get up and a time to go to bed, etc. all give children some way of predicting what will happen when. The child in turn feels more comfortable with the environment and more able to understand it and take initiative within the routine.

ESTABLISH EXPECTATIONS WHICH BOTH PARENTS AGREE ON. Parents need to discuss and reach some consensus about expectations for the child and methods of discipline to be used, etc. It does not mean they have to be carbon copies of each other. However, if the parents don't support one another and reach some agreement, the ensuing disruption of life may distort the true needs of the child and harm relationships with both parents. If one parent is very strict and the other very lenient, often the lenient one becomes more lenient (trying to offset the strictness) and the strict one becomes stricter (trying to offset the leniency), a recipe for disaster.

TAKE TIME TO CARE ABOUT LITTLE THINGS. Sometimes it is the small touches in life that indicate to us how a person really feels. Things like an extra moment patiently fixing your child's hair, stopping to look at a small hurt place, brushing the lint off the back of a child's coat, or just smiling as they walk by…all of this is important.

CULTIVATE A SENSE OF HUMOR. Learn to laugh at yourself and **with** others. Teach your children to do the same. Laughing together is important in building a sense of fun, mutuality, and understanding. Research indicates now that laughter releases endorphins into our systems and they are very good for us! Of course it is important to remember other people's feelings and never laugh at their failures or weaknesses.

REMEMBER VARIETY IS THE SPICE OF LIFE. Get away from home with the children now and then. We learn new things about life and about each other in new environments. Also things which caused friction between parent and child my not be so close at hand for a few hours or a day, e.g., chores or homework not done, arguments about going places with friends. Frequent small adventures may be more important to a child than a long vacation once a year. Use the parks, libraries, nature trails, camping areas, etc.

SPEND SOME TIME TOGETHER EACH DAY HAVING FUN. This daily dose of "delight" and shared activity of parents and all the children can not effectively be made up by a long or an expensive time together at the end of the week or month.

KEEP TRYING. Don't give up on your children. Most people have some troubles at some point in life. If you have the same thing happen to you over and over, try to see what part your own actions and mindset are playing in the situation. What can you change? Find help and support. Remember problems you have overcome in the past and think of how you worked it out. Talk with friends whose advice you respect. Counselors or ministers or doctors in your community may provide help. Good books may help. And now we have the Internet! Try to become resourceful and think of new approaches. Try to think about the problem as though it belonged to someone else. Elicit ideas from other family members. You don't have to agree in order to discuss a situation.

REMEMBER TO KEEP A GOOD BALANCE. There are many things to consider such as: life at home and life at work; things to discuss and things to overlook; things to make and things to buy; being with others and being alone; spending money and saving; trying to change things and trying to accept things the way they are; remembering the past, living in the present, planning for the future.

CHOOSING A DAY CARE PROVIDER

1. The younger your child the more effort and vigilance this requires because the baby and the toddler can not tell you what happened during the day.
2. Most communities require day care settings to be reviewed and certified by some agency. Check on this. It provides some guidelines, but you must also observe the home or facility for yourself and not assume that just because the center has an agency certification that it will meet your child's needs. Also, adults in the center or preschool should have a state police form showing they have no history of child abuse.
3. In every situation, always check for safety. Examples: no materials that are toxic left about, heaters properly enclosed so that children can not get burned, fenced area for play outside, rules for the safe use of outside and inside equipment, no broken toys about, etc. Even broken toys that don't look

dangerous should be removed.
4. Cleanliness and general order are important. Check out food preparation and serving areas and bathrooms. These may not be easily visible.
5. Check the kind of snacks and meals to be provided. Look for fresh fruits and vegetables, some good sources of protein, and whole grains. High sugar items should not be daily fare.
6. You need to know who is in charge, who are the other people taking care of your child, and what is the normal routine of the day and the general program of the home or center or school. Check to see if the head person is there each day and for how long.
7. Check to see that there is an adequate adult to child ratio. The younger the children, more adults per given number of children are needed. Actual ratios required by states may vary. If the caregiver is taking care of children with special needs, a higher ratio of teachers to children is needed also.
8. The care-giving place or preschool needs to have your phone number and how to reach you at all times. They will also need allergy information, who to call in an emergency, information and possible permission for them to have the child treated by a doctor if the parent or emergency person can not be located. This is probably not as difficult today as it was before the days of cell phones. The school may also need a change of clothing for your child.
9. Find out the protocol for how to handle concerns that the parents have or that the caregiver might have. You need a time when people are not hurried or harried and a place for necessary privacy. Check for the plan when you first are looking at the center or school. Don't wait until a problem arises.
10. Most good day care centers and home providers offer an educational program. Look around the center for good books, puzzles, blocks, paper and crayons and paints, science activities, growing plants, etc. Look for the vitality of the children being taken care of and how they are using the materials and equipment. Children need a stimulating, interesting, and active life with interaction and communication with other children and with adults.

11. Monitoring for the child's growth in all areas is essential. The availability of activities does not guarantee that each child is making good use of the opportunities.
12. Check to see how much time the children spend in front of the TV. I am opposed to young children spending large amounts of time this way to keep them quiet and entertained. Of course, there may be a short program that is okay, or even good, if it is only a small part of the child's day and if the adult talks with the child about the program. What was it about? What happened? Did you have a favorite character? etc.
13. Check to see how the environment and values of the teachers and caregivers fit with your own beliefs about what is important.
14. Find out how discipline matters are handled.
15. Talk with other parents who have used the center, school, or day care home. They are usually a good source of information about the facility, the program, and the staff.
16. Don't expect total perfection, but do expect a safe and good situation for your child. After your child is in the program, continually be vigilant as to how your child is progressing. Take time to engage your child in conversation about their experiences when you are on your way home, if it is possible. Communicate with the caregiver or teacher on a regular basis... not just when something is wrong.
17. Remember all people need confirmation that they are doing a good job... so don't forget to thank other adults who are working with your child. Often these people are going far beyond the call of duty. They may be an important influence on your child's life.

LOOKING AT THE "WHOLE DAY" OF THE CHILD

Sometimes in the hectic schedules of families today, time is not taken to access the whole day of the child. Each person is "MANAGING" their part, but because no one person is with the child all the time, maybe nobody knows or thinks about the complete day of the child.
Just by becoming more aware, parents may be able to better organize the time together in the family to include any important

things that may have been overlooked.

What do you see when you make a conscious overview of your child's day? Here is a list of some things I believe should be there.

- Moments of hugs and shared delight with the parents. These are important especially at the beginning and end of the day.
- Appropriate greetings and goodbyes to the teachers or caregivers.
- Learning and practicing little chores at home, day care, or school.
- Opportunities to watch others working and playing.
- Learning to become independent...dressing, tooth brushing, etc.
- A time to play spontaneously with other children.
- Taking responsibility to put away activities and help clean up.
- A time to hear stories read or told and to discuss them.
- Times to rest.
- Times for vigorous physical activity, usually outside.
- Opportunities to draw, paint, use modeling materials in creative ways. (See paper on Skills and Creativity in section For Parents and Teachers).
- Opportunity to learn about animals and interact with a pet.
- Participation in singing, in listening to music, moving to the music, etc.
- Times for thoughtful quiet times, for observing nature, looking at books, working puzzles, etc.
- Meal times with healthy food and an opportunity to learn table manners.
- Times for talking, not just parent to child or vice-versa, but reciprocal communication.

Comments

The reader may notice that I did not mention times for "Time Out" or times to go to your bedroom for "speaking back" (as my husband had to do as a child). So what about time for discipline? This is one subject I don't profess to know much about. My own parents disciplined mostly by having long conversations about things or by using what they thought of as a "reasonable result" from your actions. However, I can remember getting spanked when I was about five or six for not obeying their injunction to stay in the room I was in while they went into the back hall to discuss how much the sweater cost that Mother had bought for Grandmother. I had carefully snuck around to the bathroom that had a door to that back hall and I had my ear to the keyhole when they caught me! Certainly I knew right from wrong in this instance and purposely disobeyed. I remember it all. So the spanking, I believe, was deserved. I also remember that I liked my parents so much and respected them so much that this did not change my feelings toward them. Even the spanking was "not in anger" or hurtful. I think I was surprised they were clever enough to catch me! But the fact that I got caught might have kept me from further exploits in deception. Today I do not condone spanking...I just happened to remember this scenario from my childhood and thought it was interesting from a historical perspective.

    I do believe that if parents find that they are punishing a child frequently, they need to look at their expectations, how well they are teaching the child, and how they can rearrange the schedule and routine so there are less problems, etc. Seek help from people whose lives you respect and who may have dealt successfully with a similar situation. Books and professional advice are also available. Try to find children for your child to play with who are good mentors for them; children whose attitudes and behavior are in keeping with what you are teaching.

    This brings us back to the subject of looking at the whole day of the child. Sometimes by improving some things, other things that were a problem become less so. Try to find a little time in the day to spend with each child. Build a strong personal relationship with each child. One friend of mine in college told me that as a small child her dad would take her outside to look at the stars for a few moments on clear nights. She soon could find the Big Dipper and they would notice where it appeared. This took only a little time, but it was very important in her day, a special time with Dad and learning to see the beauty around us. I heard of a mother who while driving her kindergartener to school took advantage of those ten minutes to enjoy listening to her child sing a song, repeat a poem, practice addition or subtraction, or even make up a story.

Remember, during the day it is important to acknowledge your child's presence, questions, and ideas. There may not be a planned time for this, but opportunities will arise. Even if it only is a smile, a short comment, or a longer discussion, it matters. Since children are very much people who live in the present it is best to discuss and do what you can when the moment is at hand.

My last comment is about the term "MANAGING." So much in life today is about managing, getting everything properly arranged, remembering everything on the list, etc. We speak of "managed care" in the medical profession and elsewhere. I am afraid, however, that sometimes in the effort to manage efficiently we lose the "care" part of the package and a sense of the whole. It is as though we have all become one of those interchangeable manmade parts to be used in first one machine or another. In many ways we begin to dehumanize ourselves and others. We want to fit people into little prearranged cubicles. We stress getting along and being alike…so one child will do or another, one husband will do or another, one teacher will do or another, one friend can replace another…can they? Think about it. When we are that replaceable we have lost our uniqueness and all those very special qualities that make us each who we most are. I don't think anybody can replace anyone else. We have to consciously try to remain human (and not behave like a machine) as the world hurtles onward in its quest for technological perfection.

GOOD AUTHORITY

Good authority is necessary in the lives of children. Each person's authority, however, is limited, just like all good authority is. All adults are subject to the general laws of society, and the laws of society are subjected to the interpretation of judges. There are checks and balances in the family and community and schools just as there are in our government. It is incumbent upon parents to confidently assume proper roles of authority.

Good authority is respectful of the child, can discuss appropriate things with the child, yet good authority knows there are times to say yes and times to say no. The adult in charge looks at the total needs of the child and is willing to make even unpopular decisions that promote growth and development for the child.

The abdication of this role leaves the child at the mercy of his own inadequate knowledge or the push and pull of peers. This can happen for many reasons. Our modern society emphasizes freedom and equality. We tend to think that authority is bad. We wish to decrease conflict and we want our children to make choices. For these and other reasons the adult may not provide enough guidance and children may get hurt physically or socially or in other ways because they are not getting the supervision and the training they need or they are not mature enough for the choices they are given to make.

The abdication of this role of "the good authority figure" also leaves the adult in a bad situation. Since the adult is not setting many limits or taking care of the routine, rules, and structure of life, the situation may become chaotic. The children's behavior may become overwhelming to the adult. The adult may feel upset and inadequate. At some point the adult may become very frustrated and act with malice toward the child.

In the acceptance of this role as the adult or adults in charge, the parents will take the responsibility for the major routines and structures of life. This will include such things as where we live, what is offered at mealtimes, what games and pastimes are available, chores to be done, what school to attend, what TV programs to watch, religious education, etc. Many times the children's likes and dislikes can be taken into consideration among all the things that matter in weighing the issues. Good authority understands that as the person or persons in charge, they are not perfect and they need to be thoughtful and seek help when needed.

When children complain to us about a major structure or routine in life, it may be a good opportunity for us to learn more about what is going on in their lives. Sometimes the real subjects that need exploring are not those on the surface. In the listening, the adult may discover more about the child. In the discussions between parent and child, the child may learn more about the parent and more about the reasons for the structure and routine as they exist. They may also learn that they can be looking forward to a time when they will be in charge of many of the structures and routines for themselves. I frequently reminded my preschool children of this fact when they complained about certain things and didn't agree with my judgment calls.

When I was growing up over sixty years ago, many adults made judgments about what I said or did or even how I looked. Sometimes they spoke directly to me and sometimes they talked with my parents. I believe in that place and time most adults considered that a normal part of being an authority in a child's life. They would have considered themselves remiss in their duty if they had not spoken up. After all, maybe other people were not seeing the same things. The aunts, uncles, grandparents, teachers, neighbors did not expect the parents to be the only ones teaching, encouraging, and reprimanding the child when necessary.

I found it interesting as a child that when other adults complained to my parents about me or when I shared with my parents things other adults or even children had criticized about me, my parents listened dutifully to opinions of "the others," but after thinking things over and discussing what had been said, they integrated everything they knew about the situation and gave me the benefit of their thoughts on the matter. (At least that was how it seemed to me.) I think they had a good plan. They also helped me see the reasons that others might have said what they did. My parents accepted their role as the major authority in my life until I was twenty-one years old! And after that they still offered thoughtful advice at critical times.

It seems to me today that people do not want to say anything to someone else's child nor do they want to say much to the parents about the child, especially if it has negative connotations. We no longer consider ourselves an authority for the children outside our immediate families. Maybe as a result important perspectives for children and their parents are lost. I would guess there is a balance that is a good place to be. But whatever that balance is, it serves us best when everyone involved, children and adults and the broader community, have some agreement in their minds about what is appropriate. I do not think my parents questioned the appropriateness of other people's speaking out, but they often differed with their opinions and they did not hesitate to discuss the whole situation with me probably beginning when I was about five.

ASSUMPTIONS

We often assume children know what we knew when we were their age. But the life world of children is very different from what it was twenty-five or fifty years ago. And even in a similar environment, each individual is different. If we are assuming a child knows something and they don't, we may be missing golden opportunities to help them learn. It is imperative to continually observe what children know and understand and beware of making too many assumptions. Children today probably know some things we did not know at their age.

We often assume that if we give a child a directive such as, "Hand me the glass on the table," that would be an easy thing to do. We think a four- or five-year-old should be able to do that. Yet just today I asked a child to hand me something. In response, she showed me her hands. She did not understand the meaning of my request. So I said, "Oh, when I say **hand me** something that means for you to **pick it up with your hands and give it to me**." And I showed her by doing it. She complied happily. Although it actually appeared funny to me, I did not laugh because the child was trying to do what I requested and I knew that adult's laughter in a situation like that could make the child feel badly and less likely to try next time.

We also often assume that if a child has a certain piece of information that the next step is easy… like if you know the sounds of the letters then you should be able to sound out a word. However, some children have trouble sliding the sounds together and hearing the word. So playing games with this and treating it as an intriguing quest makes it easier for the child to progress than showing shock that your child can't do this.

I once knew a child who learned all the sounds and read with seeming ease sounding out words, even long words. I was shocked later to realize the child did not understand what he had been reading. So beware of your assumptions and be vigilant. Check things out along the way.

Often we assume that if a person has a visual knowledge of something like a circle that they would also be able to walk a circle or make a circle in the air. Some people may have to learn those things independently.

I remember someone telling me to keep my eyes on the music when I was learning to play the piano and I asked how I can look at the music and the keys on the piano at the same time. They did not explain it, instead they got very upset with me. I think they assumed I was being "sassy." I was being honest from my point of view. But I did not argue the points. Only years later did I learn you were not supposed to look at your fingers.

In the case of death or divorce in the family, adults may assume that once the children have made an initial adjustment that that is the end of the matter. In reality children have to readjust many times as they grow up and enter into new stages and have new questions come to mind and heart. By being observant and willing to discuss some things with our children, we can help them progress through all the different stages. Acknowledging that we don't know all the answers and that we too feel hurt and sad at times is important.

One interesting story about assumptions was told to me by a good friend. This happened to her forty years ago when she was in kindergarten. Her mother went for the first conference of the year with her teacher. The teacher told her mother that Mary only played with the boys in the block area at play time. According to the teacher, Mary showed little or no interest in joining the girls in the housekeeping area. The teacher and mother were somewhat concerned about Mary's seeming lack of interest in "girl" things. Mary told me in actuality she liked dolls and playing house...but that activity area at kindergarten seemed to have a lot of contention with everyone fussing about who was the mother or the little sister or whatever. It was the contention and the fussing that Mary had wanted to avoid! Beware of making assumptions!

RESPONSIBILITY

Learning responsibility begins early. Children see adults working and doing things that help the whole family. However, just watching other people being responsible may not be sufficient for the child to be spontaneously interested in helping. Learning how to complete chores and doing them consistently at home, school, or in day care does help the child begin to experience the satisfaction often inherent in completing tasks and helps give them a beginning sense of responsibility.

But becoming responsible is more than just completing chores. Among other things, it also means paying attention in our play or work that we don't harm others. I remember when I was seven and I almost ran my bicycle into a mother who was pushing a stroller with a baby in it. I was called to come inside and both my parents stopped what they were doing and came to the dining room table to have a big discussion with me. They talked to me for a long time about the responsibility of riding a bike and being in charge of where I was riding it and what was happening. I wanted to be a big girl and ride my bike, but they told me in no uncertain terms that if I could not be more careful and responsible, I would have to put the bike away for a long time. I think in retrospect that was a good lesson for me. I watched more carefully from then on.

Sometimes children have difficulty being responsible because the adults in their lives don't cooperate to help their efforts. Consider the question of taking care of library books. If the child has a special bag or place to keep the books and others in the family can not bother them, then the child can learn to be responsible for the books. But if no effort is made to keep younger children from taking them out and mislaying them around the house, then the older child has a hard time being responsible.

Responsibility is learned like most everything else through **example, explicit teaching**, and **practice**. Being a part of a family or group where we feel included and taken care of probably goes a long way toward helping us care about being responsible and how our actions affect others.

What am I responsible for? What are the other people in my family or work group responsible for? Sometimes people have assumptions about these things that are very different from mine. Whose job is what? All through life these things need to be discussed and adjustments made as the situations change. This is another area where our assumptions can get us in trouble.

Can a person be too responsible? The answer to this is probably yes. This is especially true if we are constantly doing other people's work for them. Usually this makes the relationship strained and people have a hard time respecting each other as a result. Of course we can help each other out from time to time. That is not the same thing as one person taking over for another.

Sometimes being super responsible means we become too hard on ourselves when things we considered "our responsibilities" don't turn out according to our expectations. As we get older and deal with more complex situations we realize that our being responsible is only one aspect of the outcome of things.

OBSTACLES TO LANGUAGE DEVELOPMENT

LACK OF CONVERSATION – For the infant, toddler, and very young child the time with a trusted adult that they talk with each day as they go through daily routines and play times is the foundation of their language development. It is easier for the child to pick up the meaning of language from persons and situations they are with consistently than from an ever-changing variety of people and situations. When adults spend time with children and know them well, the adult will pick up what the children mean by the sounds they are making and this, then, is success to the child and will encourage further language efforts. Little games that can be repeated from day to day like peek-a-boo, naming little play animals, making animal sounds, and naming things the child uses everyday such as: spoon, cup, cap, shirt, etc. are important.

TOO MUCH TV – There are many reasons to avoid spending much time in front of the TV. First and foremost is that there are many important activities that the child should be engaged in rather than sitting placidly in front of a TV. Also the images and actions on TV change fast and may promote confusion. Much of the action is shown and not described verbally as it would have been on the old radio programs that school age children used to enjoy. Thirdly, the child may find the medium mesmerizing and become accustomed to sitting and hearing and seeing passively, without understanding. It the child asks questions, other people may not like being interrupted and the child learns this and so he just sits without getting the explanation he needs. Many times adults do not watch the program and therefore cannot discuss what the child has seen or heard. Even if the child is involved in some other activity, the noise from the TV may be background noise in the house that interferes with the child's hearing clearly the everyday speech of family members. And last but not least, advertisements and programs on the TV may promote the false idea that buying and having "certain things" will make us happy.

LACK OF ROUTINE FAMILY MEAL TIMES – These were times when children learned manners such as how to say: "Please pass the peas," or "May I be excused?" They listened to adults speak and they had a chance to hear parents discussing interesting happenings of the day or they had a chance themselves to share something that had happened to them. The talking occurred in a little more formal way than at other times. The children learned to wait until one person had finished speaking before another started. This was good preparation for school and life. If families can't do this every night, then maybe they can set aside several nights a week where a meal and conversation do occur. Look for other places in the day where you can have a little conversation with children. (Many mothers and daughters in past generations had meaningful conversations while they were preparing meals and washing dishes afterwards.)

LACK OF ALERTNESS ON CHILD'S PART – Busy families often read or tell stories at bedtime. This can be a special time together and a calming way to end the day. But the child may not be listening well if he is tired. For these reasons it is important to read and tell stories at other times of the day as well. It is by having books read or stories told in a rather formal way that the child is introduced to many important words and ideas that are not used often in regular conversation. See paper on "Story Time" for more details.

ADULT FAILS TO LISTEN WITH ATTENTION – It is true that adults cannot always stop and listen to everything a child may want to say, but it is important that the child be acknowledged and know that the adult will at some point listen and talk with him or her. Knowing cues for this helps. One teacher taught me the technique of teaching the children to approach the back of my chair and put their hand on my shoulder. I could pat their hand in response to their presence and they would wait until I came to a good place to stop what I was doing with some other child. Most adults do respond to the child immediately when there is a crisis, but parents and teachers should beware of responding only when there is a crisis or only talking with a child when there is a problem.

ADULTS DO NOT KNOW HOW TO HELP THE CHILD – It is important to learn more about language development and to know when to seek professional help. It may be that a child has a hearing loss and this needs to be ascertained. Even children who do not have hearing losses may have problems in processing the sounds that they hear into correct meaning. More information about this (re: the work of Lesley Tan) can be found in the paper on Audio Processing in the next section.

LACK OF VALUE ON ORAL COMMUNICATION – Our culture often seems to value most what we wear, how we look, or what kind of house or toys we have. In many preschools the show-and-tell time is mostly "show" and little "tell." Oral speaking activities in primary schools today have diminished and other subjects take up the time. Patsy Rodenburg, in her book *The Need for Words*, makes a vibrant case for the importance of words in our lives. In chapter 2, (Rodenburg, p.19) she tells what school was like when she was a child, when teachers emphasized oral work such as group speaking, reading aloud, singing, chanting, saying a poem in front of the class, etc. She believes these were a help in overcoming her own speech impediment and also in laying the foundation for her career as a speech coach to actors and other people.

UNDERSTANDING NUMBER CONCEPTS AND LEARNING TO COUNT

Before children are formally taught counting, it is helpful if they have learned concepts concerning same and different; more and less; big, bigger, and biggest; and small, smaller, and smallest, etc. Practice comes in daily activities and conversation, e.g., "Can you please give me the biggest box in that pile?" A set of measuring cups can be set in order from the smallest to the largest. Making a nest of the measuring cups is a self-correcting activity. They won't fit together right unless they are in order.

You can make up games with things in a bag such as two items of very different sizes such as socks, balls, and spoons. Ask the child to feel inside and bring out the biggest spoon. Next ask for the little spoon. Continue with asking for each of the items left inside. To make the game easy the first time you can show the child the items you are placing in the bag and tell him the proper terms for each item as you put it in the bag; for example: the biggest spoon, the smallest spoon, the biggest ball, the smallest ball, etc. A good story to introduce these concepts is *The Three Bears.* By reading the story over and over, and emphasizing the graded sixes of the chairs, bowls, and beds, it will help the children remember the concepts.

Many folk tales are about three; e.g., **Three Little Pigs, Three Billy Goats Gruff,** and *The* **Three Bears.** If children have listened to these stories and counted out with the adult the little pigs, the goats, and bears it will be easier for them to learn to formally count. I think the best time to count the animals is at the beginning of the story or the end. It is better not to break the story line once it has begun.

Children do pick up some understanding of numbers from general happenings and discussions that they hear. But it is also helpful to teach them in some specific way and to get feedback from the child in order to know what the child understands.

Although there are many ways to teach numbers, I think some are better than others. In compiling the following suggestions for parents, I have tried to use some of my own ideas that I found useful over the years as well as some of the Montessori principles such as simplifying what you are teaching in the beginning games and activities.

In teaching numbers in the beginning, I believe it is important to say them in the normal order, e.g., one, two, three, four, five, etc. It is not necessary to introduce the Arabic symbols 1, 2, 3, etc. at first. Learning to understand that "this" is one object, or here are two objects is the basic idea. Limit your number teaching to just "one" and "two" in the beginning. For example, "Here is one spoon, one fork." "Here is one piece of cheese for you." "Have you seen the two dogs that are in our front yard?" Use opportunities during the day where counting one, or counting out one, two is helpful. Be sure your child understands and uses the numbers you have been teaching him correctly before you introduce the next number. To check out understanding, you can have the child bring you "one" of something that you need or "two" of something. Be sure in your counting activities that you use the same objects in any one group such as the two spoons or two crackers. Don't add together unlike things such as apples and oranges.

After the child gets one and two right all the time, teach three. For example, you can demonstrate counting out three crackers and putting them in a row on a napkin. Then the child can count out three for his/her napkin and for another child's napkin. Repeating the same thing immediately helps the child's memory. If necessary the adult can whisper the numbers with the child as he tries to say them. Then you can comment that, "Yes, they each have three." Use the number three often with your children until you are sure they understand the concept and can consistently count to three. Can you hand me one block, two blocks, three blocks, etc.

Children need to understand one-to-one correspondence; in other words when you are counting you only count each item once. Sometimes children can say the numbers in order correctly (which is an important learning), but they do not understand one-to-one correspondence. Usually they will get the idea if you point it out and demonstrate and also tell them that you are touching each item only once.

I think it is questionable to teach children telephone numbers or other numbers out of order before they can count to ten in the normal order. In some cases this might interfere with learning the regular sequence. Try to remain low-key if your child says the numbers in the wrong order. Do not laugh at this or make fun of it or call attention to it. This can be problematic. Sometimes the child repeats this to get everyone to laugh and this reinforces a bad pattern of trying to be silly (with things that should be serious) to get attention. Also as mentioned before, it may make learning correct numerical order more difficult. For most children this might not be a problem and they would sort it out in time, but why take the chance and cause confusion if not necessary?

In this paper I did not try to explain how to teach the written Arabic symbols 1, 2, 3, at the same time a young child is learning to count. In our Montessori school we taught the symbols using felt number symbols that the child could feel and we taught the meaning of the symbol at the same time by counting out blocks. However, the child had had many previous activities to help him be ready for this. (See Section VI for more information on this.)

If, as the parent, you find you are getting frustrated with your child when you try to teach, it may be that your child needs more preparatory activities and it is always best to back up to activities and little games that the child and parent can do successfully without undue stress. Continue to interact with your child and spend time with her/him. Teach little skills that promote the use of hands, the understanding of procedures, and remembering the little steps in various activities. There are many things to do that will help lay the foundation for understanding numbers. Check your library for books or on the Internet for supplementary activities.

SHORTCUTS

We live in a world of short cuts, prefabrication, etc. We want a quick, easy, efficient solution. We have become accustomed to the era of mass production and technology, management and goal setting. We want everything in an understandable "pay-for-able" chunk. But if we only deal with those types of phenomena, we indeed lose much.

I do not believe that there is a good shortcut for the majority of things. Many important accomplishments reflect lifelong commitments. Our children are not fully raised in eighteen years. Our minds are not completely educated in twelve years or sixteen or even seventy! Our health and fitness depend upon our everyday continual exercise, good eating, spiritual life, and managing stress as well as our genes and modern medicine! The best use of our talents results from significant time spent in study and practice.

There is more out there than meets the eye or hand or ear in our experiences. We often see only the tip of the iceberg. In every home or classroom there are things happening that are not easy to observe. On the long road to anywhere there are many other things happening that we learn from. On the short road, we may think we reached the end goal, but we certainly did not have the same journey.

The religions of the world have emphasized the long road of life and values that are important generation after generation. They also emphasize things that are not easy to see such as what is in our hearts. They help us understand life from a different point of view than the utilitarian and short-term one that is so common in our culture today. Many people have left the faith of their ancestors. Some are consciously seeking a meaningful religious life that fits with their personal beliefs. But some people may be seeking a **shortcut** to happiness in the icons of modern culture. How sad!

I guess there are times and places that shortcuts are helpful and useful. Most often it is when we know a lot about something and we are very skilled. Then we can leave out certain steps or think up a better way of doing something that does not impact the final outcome negatively. When I studied sewing in college, I had already been sewing for about eight years. I found that the methods being used to teach beginning students included a lot of basting and stay-stitching. I left out a certain amount of that without dire results. Other examples are some of the excellent cooks who do not take the time to measure with a spoon exactly. They have been doing this for so long and so successfully that the pinch of this and dab of that works fine for them. In a sense both of these examples given are not really shortcuts because the individual had already practiced on the long road of experience. In conclusion, think carefully and be aware of what you may be losing when you take a shortcut in trying to reach any major goal.

CONTRASTS

I think children learn a lot through contrasts. This is hot, this is cold. Today is colder than yesterday, so we have to wear a heavier coat, etc. Commenting about the contrasts of life and helping children learn to observe for these is very important.

It is also easier to notice and remember strong contrasts than things that are more alike. This is one of the reasons that stories, passed down from generation to generation before writing, used strong contrasting imagery. Examples are: the big bad dragon, the beautiful princess, the little bitsy Billy Goat Gruff, the mean, ugly troll. Also remember how Little Red Riding Hood commented on the way Grandmother's eyes, ears, nose, and mouth contrasted so greatly with her memories of Grandmother.

In the early part of the previous century, children were expected to behave differently in different situations. There was a contrast in the way they dressed for play, for school, for church, and in each instance the behavior expected in each situation was different. In spontaneous play, especially if no adults were watching and listening, you saw, heard, and learned a lot about things you never saw or heard about in your home, in the classroom or in church. Also your peers judged you by what they considered important, which was different from the way adults thought. Children needed to pay attention to each situation they were in to know how to survive and thrive.

During my childhood (ages five to ten especially) in the relatively unsupervised play outside in my neighborhood, we could make lots of noise, run and jump, throw balls, climb trees, play tag, skate on the sidewalk, etc. It was not necessary to always "act nice" and certainly everybody was not always nice to me. And nobody told the adults all about this because this was a child's world not privy 100% to adults any more than their world was to us. But in general the children we played with had the same limits and guidelines for their behavior that we had learned. So although the "play" with these kids was not always happy, it was interesting and challenging and kept you alert and thinking. In retrospect it seems that it had a lot in common with much of the rest of life!

There was also the strong contrast of when to be quiet and when it was okay to talk, giggle or laugh, etc. There were rules you learned as a child about dinner table behavior. There were rules you learned about how to behave in the car or in a store with your mother, or how to act in a bus. And in my case there were lots of things to remember about Grandmother's house. We were to be "more quiet" than we were at home, to always ask before we picked up anything, to remember to say please and thank you and to give Grandmother a kiss before we left. Grandmother seemed very old. Somehow I knew and sensed a connection with her and the love that she had for me even though she never seemed to say much. In retrospect, the fact that she dressed like a very old person emphasized that she was in a different stage of life than my mother or my aunt. Today most grandmothers dress like everyone else; blue jeans and sweatshirts are a common uniform.

In my childhood, age had its privileges. There were a few societal rules about that. Children who were old enough to understand were expected to calm down in front of the elderly. The elderly were not expected to adjust to children's racing around or yelling. I was expected to make an effort to be respectful and to remember varying behaviors for varying places. I was often cued ahead of time about appropriate behavior in a new situation. In my family, the "rules" were strong suggestions and hopes and expectations more than something set in cement that would result in dire punishment if you forgot. (However you might be subjected to a long conversation about it all if you needed help in remembering.)

Yesterday I was having a visit with an old friend who complained to me that her great-grandchildren were not learning table manners. She said her grandchildren did not bother to have family sit-down meals, so the little children did not know how to use eating utensils properly. Other manners seemed likewise unknown to them. They went around touching things, looking in drawers, picking up stuff when they came to visit her. My friend felt that her own negative feelings about the children's behavior were now interfering with the feelings of love and connectedness she had hoped to have with the little children. She also noticed she was beginning to feel strained in her relationship with her grandchildren who seemed unaware of the situation. I think she did not want to discuss this with anyone for fear they would pick it up as criticism and not come back to visit.

Because so much in society has changed and both parents are often busy with work, it may be that parents have to think more consciously about teaching their children how to behave in a wide variety of situations of which they are now a part or soon will be. Behavior that is okay in one time and place may contrast sharply with what is okay in another situation. Discussing this in explicit ways and providing opportunities for children to practice what they are learning is important. Children often don't automatically pick up these ideas. Parents need to know reasonable behaviors that children of different ages can usually learn. Openly **criticizing and nagging** children for not behaving in a certain way that you **assumed** they would know often leads to feelings of discouragement and failure and sometimes rebellion. As a result the children are not motivated to want to cooperate and improve behavior. Teaching and practice are what helps.

My mother had a cousin known as Cousin Lotte. When she and her husband came home on furlough from serving as missionaries in Cuba they would often come and visit us. Cousin Lotte made no bones about complaining to my mother about the lack of manners of the children in the United States. Mother, taking a cue from that, decided that we should all learn more formal manners and we began the playing the game, "Cousin Lotte is Here!" It was uproarious fun and we enjoyed exaggerating the greetings and salutations and how to eat more correctly or whatever. My brother George made the funniest faces ever. Mother herself joined in the levity. However, we practiced the protocol and we got the message.

THE IMPORTANCE OF SINGING – written May, 2003

Last Sunday on Mother's Day I asked my adult Sunday school class to share with the group how they thought their mothers helped them to grow up strong. Many characteristics were mentioned, but the one that surprised and delighted me the most had to do with singing. Many people mentioned that their mothers sang around the house while they worked. One person sang for the class the cowboy song that had been her mother's favorite. She remembered every word and also the tune and she is not noted herself as a singer. One person said her mother could dance an Irish jig also! Some people said that their mothers sang favorite hymns. When a person spoke of the mother's singing I noticed a certain joy. Many of the mothers described had not had an easy life in the early part of the last century; there was lots of work, many children, little money, etc. Nobody tried to explain how the songs helped them become strong. It must have appeared self-evident.

Sudie Doughton Mason

Today while I was waiting for our boat to get fixed at a marina in Sidney, British Columbia, Canada, I picked up the Sunday *Times Colonist* newspaper and found an article about Pat Carfra, who is known as the "Lullaby Lady." This write-up told about her work emphasizing the importance of singing with infants and children. This information arrived for me right on the heels of hearing the people in the Sunday school class talk about their mothers' singing. Carfra, originally a public health nurse, had found in her work with young mothers that many people no longer sing very much to their babies and young children. All the experiences she has had with infants and children have confirmed for her the value of singing. Carfra mentions that today we often have become passive listeners to music rather than making music ourselves. "The Lullaby Lady" believes that what parents have to offer young children in their own voices and their own songs is of inestimable worth. Carfra calls lullabies "a multi-layered experience," ("Pat Carfra, The Lullaby Lady", *Times Colonist,* May 20, 2003.)

Aha! Here is something that parents and other caregivers can do that should not be difficult at all. Sing! Sing lullabies when putting your baby to bed at night or nap time. Sing while you are about other tasks. Sing the songs you love the best over and over. Make up your own songs. Sing songs that people whom you loved sang to you. It is almost like we are tapping into a spiritual realm. It probably is comforting to both the adult and the child. And the child can hear you still singing as you work in some other part of the house. He or she knows you are there. Don't worry about having a wonderful voice, just sing.

I tried to think of examples I have from my own experiences with singing and children. I remember the funny little nonsense nursery rhyme that my own mother used to sing to my baby sister, "Go to sleep now my pumpkin, tumpkin, your sweet toes. If you sleep well, my pumpkin, you will turn to a rose." I used to sing this to my own preschoolers as they rested with heads on the table before snack time. Tears would frequently come to my eyes as the song brought back memories of my mother and little sister. In those moments I would feel a special closeness to the children in my class, and maybe they to me. Another reason I liked this lullaby for my three-, four-, and five-year-olds was because it did not call the child "a baby."

Subjects Dear To My Heart

I remember my friend Margaret Becker telling of singing to her preschoolers while they rested. She said she had a good friend who had a very good voice and sang folk songs and played the guitar. She invited the friend to come over to sing for her children at rest time. After the guest left, the children looked up and said, "Now, Mrs. Becker, will you sing for us?" Certainly this is an indicative reminder that when the person we love sings to us, something very special is shared and no amount of "better quality music" can provide that same thing.

When I was first in Chile working at a big day care center, I felt alone and often didn't know exactly what to do so I would go to the room for the *gua-guas* (infants) and just sing to the babies in the playpens. Of course neither the staff nor the babies understood my English but it was a comfort to me to have something to do that seemed right and natural and was not difficult. The babies seemed to like it.

I heard a story many years ago that has to do with the power of singing combined with love. It is the story of a tiny newborn baby that was very sick and hovering between life and death in a special care unit of the hospital. The parents had an older child that used to sing to the baby every night before the child was born. The "big sister" begged to see the tiny baby. The doctors agreed to let the sister in to see the baby. As the child came near the infant, she started to sing the little song that she had sung for so many nights. As the staff watched, the baby's heart rate improved. Every day they allowed the child in to sing. The little baby survived.

I am sure many people have written about the importance of singing. There is probably even scientific research to back it up. But like so many things in life, it seems to take a certain confluence of events to bring a subject to our conscious awareness in a strong enough fashion that we really think about it and try to do something about it. I knew some of this before, but now I see it more clearly. As I edit these papers as the older person I am becoming, I wonder if singing every day, even just to myself, might bring joy to me. I think I'll try it.

Sudie Doughton Mason

FOR PARENTS AND TEACHERS

SKILL ACTIVITIES AND CREATIVE ACTIVITIES-
THE IMPORTANCE OF BOTH

Young children need both skill-type activities and creative-type activities. They represent the use of different thought processes, all of which are needed in life. I studied creativity for many years and I loved the children's creative activities. After my Montessori education I became acutely aware of the value also of skill type activities for children. **In my early teaching in the 1960s, I had some little children who did not seem to feel confident with creative art activities, and in the 1990s, I had some children who did not want to learn things by procedure and practice.** This paper is an effort to see the benefits of both creative and skill-based activities and to make some of their differences and similarities understandable to the reader.

Skill-type activities are basically things the child will be doing over and over, like brushing teeth, washing hands, using a knife, using scissors, pouring, setting a table, holding a pencil, tying a bow, etc. Teaching skills by showing the child specific procedures to follow can help the child learn the skill and also promote the development of **attention to detail, sequential thinking, and memory.** Skill activities usually have a distinct beginning and end. (Practical Life Activities in Montessori emphasize this same type of teaching.)

Of course, there may be different levels of any one skill. It takes practice to master a skill. After working on something, the child will improve and be ready to begin the activities of the next level. I think it is satisfying to the child and to adults to have some things we do each day where we can easily see what was accomplished. That is why it is good to have the activity simplified and the procedures to accomplish it known to the child. Mastering each level will mean the child will be more likely to be successful at the next, e.g., learn to cut short, straight lines first, then longer straight lines, then short, slightly wavy lines and so on. Three-year-olds usually are drawn to this activity. Three-year-olds love to cut for the joy of cutting. They like to put all the pieces in a little envelope to take home. It is the perfect time to learn these skills, before the need arises to use them in crafts and more complicated projects!

I have found that if you begin teaching and demonstrating skill-type activities to three-year-olds, they generally will catch on without a lot of discussion. Most three-year-olds I have known have an open mind and confidence to try. They become engaged with the activity and find it satisfying. When they are older, they may not have a "natural interest" in the procedure for these things as their interest may now be in other areas.

Creative activities for young children are those in which the child can manipulate the materials and make something, or work with something, in a way that reflects their uniqueness and developmental stage. With creative activities the children are encouraged to **enjoy the experimentation and to use their imagination.** In contrast to the skill-focused activity, **the creative activity has no "end product" that has to be a certain way.** The final product seems to evolve with a life of its own as the child works with the situation or the materials. Most young children are more interested in the process of creating than in the final product. That emphasis needs to be respected. Calling too much attention to the final product may interfere with other aspects of their creative work. Drawing with crayons on a blank paper, working with markers or crayons on blank paper, playing with play dough, painting at the easel, putting a collage together are all examples of activities which offer opportunity for creativity unless the adults try to tell the children specifically what to do and how to do it.

I felt that certain activities such as crayon drawing on blank paper and painting at the easel were well-suited to be creative activities. I did not try to tell the children what to do or how to do it with those media. In our Montessori classroom where we had many follow-the-procedure activities, the crayons and paper and the painting at the easel were very important vehicles for creative growth and expression. I think the children (albeit unconsciously) enjoyed the contrast of the type of thinking involved in the creative activity with the type of thinking in the skill- based activity.

Some social/play activities may also be creative. Examples of this might be play with unit blocks, dramatic play in a house corner, and play with sand. The children are using their minds to think up things to do or say and they are rearranging the materials and affecting the social situation and play in different and unique ways. And as with other creative activities, it is not known how it will all turn out. However, because those activities usually involve other children in a spontaneous and constantly changing situation, it may be social and interesting, but not necessarily creative for every child. A child's ability to carry out his/her creative ideas may be greatly influenced by the other children in the play area.

I think children should have opportunities to do creative art work occasionally at a different time from the general activity "hour" when the social/creative playthings like blocks, house play area, etc. are also available. Some children who are more attracted to the social play may not ever do much in the creative art area or vice versa unless they are available at separate times.

I believe the best bet is to start both skills and creative experiences early. As the child gets older, probably in the kindergarten year, it is good to discuss the differences and the similarities in these various types of activities and why it is important to be able to work both ways.

CRAFTS

Crafts activities provide children with an opportunity to make a particular thing that is often preplanned by the teacher. An example of the finished project can be shown to the children. Frequently the teacher can demonstrate the sequence of activities in making the project. Often several skills are used. Completing the project to the best of each child's ability is the main idea. Often there is opportunity in the craft for the children to use some of their own ideas in a creative fashion! The teacher may need to emphasize following the instructions to begin with and then she may need to point out the part of the project that the children can decorate "their way."

One of my favorite Christmas crafts was a Yule log made with a slice of a small log, a wad of play dough placed in the center of the piece of wood, and a candle in the middle of the play dough. The last part of the project was placing nuts, seeds, cloves, and little pinecones in the play dough all around the candle. After watching the teacher demonstrate, the children chose the color play dough they preferred, the color candle they wanted, and then they preceded with the project. The completed Yule logs were all different due to the variety in color combinations and in the various arrangements of the nuts, seeds, etc. (I learned this activity either while teaching in the Co-Op Preschool or at Head Start.)

Remember crafts are best used after a child has developed some skills, not as a starting place for learning a skill. The choice of any particular craft needs to be gauged by the ability of the children in the group to successfully complete the project in a reasonable amount of time without undue frustration for the children and teacher. If the adult takes over and does most of the craft for the child, the craft has not served its purpose. This would be an interesting discussion among experienced teachers as to how to handle the situation when a child is having difficulty. I personally would help the child with some of a project if necessary. Then in a nonchalant way, I would comment on the part I had helped with and on the part the child had done. I think it is important for the child to grasp his part in something, be proud of that, and also to acknowledge another person's part in the finished product if that is the case. I don't think it is a good idea to pretend to make something all by yourself when you didn't.

Also remember that the purpose of crafts is different from that of the creative activities; **do not use crafts in place of creative activities. If a craft is called creative, examine it to see in what way it is creative.** The word creative is not always used appropriately. We need to observe and try to understand how all these activities help the child develop. It is my guess that creative activities, skill activities, and crafts are all important in their own right as discussed earlier and yet they may also be important in some kind of broader and synergistic way.

In conclusion, I feel the best crafts for preschoolers provide a chance to follow a simple plan, an opportunity to utilize skills the child has already learned, and a place for the child's own unique decoration in color or design or in some other elaboration. (See additional crafts listed in Part VI.)

NOTES ABOUT VARIOUS ART MEDIA

The **easel** was one of the most loved activities for the young children I taught. The bright liquid colors respond to the brush of the child. Sometimes the colors drip a little; they are easily swished from here to there to make delightful abstract or stylized large pictures. Fairly large brushes make it possible to paint a lot of space fairly quickly. At the beginning of the year, I only had one or two jars of color and each color had its own brush. I did not fill the jars very full at the beginning of the year when the children tend to muddy the colors fairly fast. That way the paints were used up readily and fresh paint is added to the jar so that each child is using fairly pure colors. I put out more colors at a time as the year went along. Usually in the spring, I introduced pastels. I tried to vary the sizes and stiffness of brushes after the first several months of school. The children's paintings were a special joy to them and to me.

Painting at the easel also offered the chance to teach the child care of materials, how to hang up the finished painting, and procedures for clean-up. It also provided opportunity for children to help each other. One of my mothers commented one time that she noticed in the clean-up at the end of the day it was kind of like finger painting as the children washed the easel with various size sponges and made circles and stripes in the process!

Markers are also usually bright and bold, but they are totally different from the easel painting. The lines the children make with them are smaller and more exact than those made with the brushes at the easel. Very young children like to color on top of their first marks so this may not be the best media for the child's early endeavors since the extra heavy ink concentration may tear the paper. Also, very young children may have trouble taking off the tops and putting them back on. The struggle with that can interfere with the joy of creation. Certainly the markers are effective for certain kinds of projects, such as those where bright colors for relatively small areas are needed fast. Be sure the markers are child-safe and that the children are taught to put the lids on so that they don't dry out.

Crayons are very good as a beginning marking and drawing material for young children, especially the large crayons. The amount of pressure on the crayon will change the look of the mark. This is not possible in the same way with markers because the ink and the felt tip tend to leave a similar mark that is not greatly affected by slight changes of pressure. So for the purpose of developing the muscles in the hand and providing opportunity for the child to vary the strength and brightness of his designs and pictures, the crayons or colored pencils are better. **Colored pencils** may be hard for a very young child, but usually four-year-olds can learn to use them for some things. Relatively soft, thick-colored pencils are easier for the children to use.

Watercolors have surprised me in their appeal to young children. I did not use them with young children until the second half of my career. Later when I did try them, I found that many children learned quickly how to clean the brush between colors, and they seemed to enjoy the medium. I found some small brushes that had rather stiff bristles; I thought these worked better for the children than brushes that came with the sets. The fact that the watercolors are translucent and that one color does not hide the other but rather easily makes a new color from the combination makes them unique. Some paints for the easel combine to some extent to make new colors, but the overall impressions from tempera and watercolors are quite different.

I think the first time I tried watercolors with preschoolers I had bought some watercolors that were in separate little pots. That way in the introduction to watercolors, the children only had two or three colors and a little water for their first projects. Also, since the colors can be bought separately, the school can buy more of the colors that tend to get used up first. Later I experimented with many different kinds of sets and I liked them all but found children liked some of them better than others, but not all children preferred the same sets.

One of my favorite watercolor projects was introduced to me by Susan Lynch-Ritchie, a long-time friend and professional in the area of Early Childhood. To begin the activity the children are given a piece of heavy, white construction paper. They use a black permanent marker for the outline of their design or special object such as a house, person or monster! (Most of the permanent markers are not child safe; they cannot be left in the room for general activities. I brought them out for this special project and I kept a watchful eye on the children. After the children made the outlines, I collected the markers.) Next, I passed out a little palette of watercolors to each child. They used these to complete their picture. Some children wanted to fill various outlined areas with the colors. Others wanted to make splashes of color here and there, which gave a unique abstract quality to the design. Other children did a variety of things such as adding sky or grass or a rainbow. They were always creative and lovely.

At Susan's day care and preschool she has a special table set up with liquid water colors in little transparent containers, each with a separate brush. Her children paint with the watercolors often. She has experimented and found out what works best with her children and with this medium.

Each kind of modeling material also provides the child with a unique experience. **Play dough,** if it is a good consistency, works well for very young children because they can manipulate it fairly easy. I had to try out different recipes in different places that I lived to come up with one that worked and lasted well in each place. **Plasticine,** a synthetic modeling material, may work well with some children in some settings. It tends to be hard to begin with, but after the child works it for a while it is more pliable. It will hold a shape better than most play dough does. Although Plasticine is a particular brand, there are other similar materials on the market. It is important to check for a product that is "child-safe."

Real clay is my favorite modeling material, but it is difficult to keep it at the right consistency and it requires more clean-up than play dough. Most children now seem to like real clay and seem intrigued with working with it. Its textures and three-dimensional qualities are wonderful. I do remember some children I worked with who didn't like it because it was "dirty looking" or messy and even some teachers and parents who didn't particularly appreciate it. It can make a terrible smell if left to mold in the back of some cabinet! (I know from personal experience.) I have often wondered if the nondescript color of real clay is somehow important because the child is drawn to what he is doing and making and there is no bright color distracting him. As a part of the human race, people have a long history of using natural clay for both utilitarian and creative projects. I have always felt a deep and satisfying connection with natural materials such as clay, wood, stones, etc. Many children seem to like them too.

I think the main thing to remember is that children interact with each of the media previously discussed in different ways. Providing only one or two materials for creative art work is not giving the child the variety that is easily available and that might be helpful. I do not mean to imply that children need a choice of all of the media at the same time. Actually, limiting what is available at any one time may help children try out media that they have not used or enjoyed in the past. Often children will always use the markers and never use the crayons, or always use the paints and never the colored pencils, etc.

SAVING CHILDREN'S ART WORK

Parents of my school children were often in a quandary about what to do with all their children's art work. Of course they tried to post some of the most recent things on the refrigerator or in some other special places. One mother kept her children's previous works in a large plastic container in the basement. She still has them although her children are now in college. Another parent said she saved everything for several months and then she would make a video of the work.

Many people probably don't have the time and energy and interest to save everything or keep a complete record, but it might be wise to keep some examples of each child's work for each year of their childhood. It could be done in notebook or scrapbook or folder form. Photographs of pictures, collages, mobiles, sculptures, and other projects could be kept in place of the originals. Having the child in the picture with some of the works is a great idea too.

It is important to put the name of the child and the year on any project that is to be kept. We have many wonderful Christmas decorations that were made by our children when they were young, but at the time we did not write the name of each child and the year on each one. Now when I put these decorations on my tree, I wish I knew for sure who had made each one and when!

I will close this section on children's art with a reminder of how special it is and how important it is for each child to express his or her ideas in his/her own way with art media. Remember, children's **"art has nothing to do with skill, exactitude, or even faithful repetition and copy of nature,"** (Wilhelm Voila, *Child Art and Frank Cizek*, p. 9). For further thoughts on this read more about Cizek's work, study Lowenfeld or other art books mentioned in the Bibliography. There is also a discussion in Part VII concerning my answers to questions about the children's creativity in our Montessori school that relates to these subjects.

ART APPRECIATION

I believe that children's first appreciation of art comes from enjoying their own art work. As children explore the various media they realize that pictures can be drawn and painted in different ways. They often like to watch their friends drawing and painting also. I believe that there is a natural connection between children and art just as there is with music and spoken language. It is a part of the rich heritage of being a human being.

Children's growing appreciation of art work in general comes from many sources. By studying the illustrations in children's books they can get a sense of the power and potential variety in pictures. I have books illustrated with block prints, collages, pen and ink, watercolors, etc. These can be pointed out to the children and the different kinds of illustrations can be compared with each other as to their various visual characteristics and to the impressions they leave with us. The illustrations in a child's picture book are as important to me as the story. Many classic children's books have authors who are both illustrators and authors. Many of those people were artists before they wrote children's books!

Another way children grow in their appreciation of art is by studying classic works. Betty introduced the art postcard program that goes with **Aline D. Wolf's book,** *Mommy, It's a Renoir,* to our Montessori children. The children immediately liked her presentations; they enjoyed matching the pictures and studying them. They liked learning the names of some of the most famous artists and pictures. The children were soon able to notice which paintings were by the same artist. They had become aware of line, color, medium, style, etc. without explicitly talking about it. Several parents mentioned to me that their children had told them the name of a painting when the family saw a replica of it somewhere. I was amazed at the interest the children had in this program and how good their memories were from one presentation to the next, which was a least a week later.

WORK AND PLAY

The general classifications of work and play often bring ideas to people of good and bad or fun and drudgery. These stereotypes can limit our thinking. I believe all of us need both work and play. We probably should learn many types of play as well as learning many ways to work.

I have asked some older adults what they remember about how they spent their time before they went to school. They remember helping with chores around the house, folding, dusting, setting the table, etc., whatever Mother, Father, Grandparent, or other adult in charge of the children wanted to have them do. These same adults told me that they played a lot also and that playing often was outside, rearranging boxes and playing store or other imaginary play.

I have a collection of old primers and readers. In these books, examples of play might be: play with a ball, roll a hoop, play with dolls, climb trees, play patty-cake with baby, etc. Illustrations in these books show children working in many ways: sewing, weeding a garden, feeding animals, sweeping the hearth, rocking the baby's cradle. The lessons at school were also considered work. Music lessons and practice were work. Playing the piano for fun was play.

Maybe some of the play activities left more room for the child's own ideas and imagination; perhaps the work activities taught the child to follow a given sequence and perfect a skill. However, many play activities such as marbles and other games require the development of skills and following the rules of the game, while some work activities may also need the child's ideas and imagination.

When I think about children's playing "kick the can" and climbing trees for fun in my childhood, I remember thinking that

I was a klutz at those activities and I did not like them. If I wanted to play, I would get a set of crayons and draw or find a friend to help me make up stories and put on little productions. I wanted to do well in my activities; I tended to steer clear of most sports or games I thought I would show up my "below par" ability. As a result of my experiences and feelings, I think that children often need to be helped and encouraged in any area that is difficult for them, work or play. I think my teachers and parents tended to think if something is mostly play than it is not so important how well the child does in it. Maybe that isn't true any more. And maybe I am wrong about what they thought.

Observing children at work and play can teach us a lot about a child. Is the child concentrating on the activity? Does the child persist in the activity? Does the child show resourcefulness in problem solving? Is the child using memory? Is the child willing to play and work at things which are not so easy for him or her? Does he/she move into more complicated forms of the activity that make use of some of skills learned earlier? In what ways does the play involve others?

It seems to me from watching and sometimes participating in "play" on the playground at school when I was a child, that true give and take and sharing of ideas on the playground was often not happening. Instead, one or two children were doing the thinking and planning in the group and the others were expected to follow. A pecking order was often quickly established. We need to be aware that our assumptions about what is going on in a "play setting" may be different from what is happening, just as our assumptions about other things are often not 100% correct.

THOUGHTS ABOUT FUN FOR CHILDREN

I have noticed that in the world of many preschool parents and teachers and the makers of activities for little children, the first consideration about an activity is, "will it be fun?" Or if the activity is something important and needed from the adult's point of view, then the question becomes, "how can we make it fun?" The importance of fun probably reached its apex in the late '70s and '80s.

Subjects Dear To My Heart

I do not remember any mention of "fun" as being of major importance in my early Child Development classes in the '50s and '60s. Indeed, at that time we strove to keep a low-key, calm environment. We did not want the children to get excited. (I think fun often begets excitement.) We offered the children a wide variety of activities to help them learn about things in their immediate environment and to facilitate their social and physical development. Maybe the enthusiasm for fun developed in some part as a reaction to the rather staid environment in some nursery schools of the '40s and '50s.

Although "fun" may not have the same prominent status among professionals that it had several decades ago, many teachers and parents may still be unconsciously affected by the desire to provide lots of fun. Unless their consciousness has been raised about this, many people who received their education in the "fun era" may feel unsuccessful if the children are not having fun.

What is fun? According to the dictionary it means to be merry, to joke around. It implies a certain amount of levity. I agree we all need some fun every day. We even know scientifically now that laughter and fun are important in releasing the endorphins in our blood that help keep us healthy. But like so many things in life, it is important, but only part of the story. I believe children's needs are far more complex than just fun and games.

Children want us to recognize in them all the complexities of their lives, just as we want to be seen by our friends as total people, not just an icon of some abstraction or generalization. I once read where a man said that as a young boy he found great hope in the pictures of children from the Bible stories. His grandmother had a book with stories and beautiful illustrations. It was in these pictures that he first saw children depicted as serious and important people. He says that made a big impression on him, and he began to take his own childhood life as more important.

Sometimes in my classroom children would come over at activity time and tell me they were bored. I tried to look behind the word to see what they were really saying to me. Were they saying they were tired and needed to rest? Were they saying they weren't being stimulated or excited or **having fun**? I tried to resist the temptation to provide an immediate solution to the problem. Sometimes just by listening calmly or suggesting they rest or watch a lesson was helpful. Soon they would be up and about choosing an activity.

An overemphasis on fun activities provided by the adults in the preschool years may give a false view of what life and school in particular are all about. We seem to live in a society that tries to sell us happiness and offers joy and fun with each new product. The products become bigger, better, or fancier as the need for happiness and joy seems to continue unabated and unsatisfied. So the "fun thing" is multiplied many times over in our general culture. Parents and teachers need to help children see beyond the hype of advertisement and to learn to appreciate things in life that may truly be related to joy and happiness both now and in the future.

And what might those things be? Family life, nature experiences, interesting work, growing things, arts and crafts, friendships, participating in sports and games, helping others, music, spiritual development, books, poetry, and learning new things. I believe people need to eventually answer this question for themselves.

AUDITORY PROCESSING AND
THE WORK OF LESLEY TAN

Auditory Processing is a subject hearing and speech specialists have known about for a long time. It has to do with taking in correct meaning from spoken words. It is important for teachers and parents to know something about it because if a child has difficulty in this area it may affect behavior, learning, and many other things. There are ways that parents and teachers can help a young child who is not yet processing language as correctly and quickly as some of his or her peers.

I was indeed fortunate to be at Betty Nicholson's house the day that the series of four small books about Auditory Processing arrived from Australia. They were from Betty's dear friend Lesley Tan. Betty and Leslie had become friends when they were teachers in Indonesia many years ago.

The book, *Auditory Processing and the Under Sixes*, no. 4 in the series, immediately caught my attention. I am sure I have known some children who might have been helped by the strategies discussed in this book. I have read further about AP from other sources, but I did not find the material as understandable and practical with their advice for parents or teachers of young children as Leslie's books are.

One of the reasons knowing about AP delay (Tan, *AP and the Under Sixes,* p.13), is because many adults assume, sometimes falsely, that children of certain ages do understand what is said to them. The adults may be critical of the child for not paying attention or not complying with instructions. The child may be getting some parts of the message, but not the whole meaning. And of course the children are responding to what they thought the message was; the child has no way of knowing that he does not fully understand the communication. Tan also notes that "AP ability normally matures to adequate levels with time." (pp. 24, 25) To order or get information about Tan's books contact her by e-mail: admin@listeningworks.com.au. Tan has graciously given me permission to quote the following.

Summary of Advice (Lesley Tan, *Audio Processing and the Under Sixes,* pp. 24, 25.)
- *Gain the child's attention before beginning the message.*
- *Use short sentences and allow time for processing.*
- *Watch the child: shorten the message if she looks uncertain.*
- *Make instructions and explanations short and simple. Give the main message directly without unnecessary preliminary phrases.*
- *For a message with several parts, plan how to break it up. Make the order logical, allow time between the parts.*
- *Give one instruction at a time. Give it in several parts if it is long.*
- *When you ask a question, give the child time to think.*
- *Be patient, allow the child time to comply with reasonable requests. If you repeat your message, shorten it if you can.*
- *When you talk, reduce noise, or wait for quiet. Otherwise, get close to the child and let her look at you.*
- *Turn the TV or radio off when no one is listening. Constant talking does not help a child to talk better.*
- *Use the child's speech as a guide for talking. If he talks in two word phrases, he will learn best from 2 or 3 words at a time.*
- *Remember that auditory processing difficulties could have distorted*

previous language or social learning and experience.
- *Give special help with social interactions. Teach the child useful short phrases for social interactions. Explain with few words.*
- *Use non-verbal ways to develop ideas and to convey feelings.*
- *Children misunderstand what is said more often than adults realize.*
- *Children who are clever or talk well can have listening difficulties.*
- *Think carefully about the way you are talking with a young child.*
- *Do not ask children if they heard you or understood. They say yes to avoid trouble. They cannot know if they heard something different from what was actually said.*
- *Look at the child closely as you talk to see if he has understood, and continue to watch to see what he does.*
- *Be positive – avoid criticism and embarrassment. Success and praise are the best motivators for further effort.*
- *For groups of children follow these word limits: 2 or 3 words for the very young (or those not talking in sentences), 6 or 7 words for kindergarten, 8 or 9 words for the first year of school.*
- *Develop and use routines – reduce the need for constant listening.*
- *Read books and stories using short phrases with frequent pauses.*
- *Use short sentences with pauses for any child who is overactive, has developmental delay, has poor language, or is unfamiliar with English.*
- *Children with AP delay may have a problem with learning two languages, but not always.*
- *Auditory processing difficulties may look like hearing problems due to ear conditions. Some children have both conditions.*
- *If hearing loss is suspected, get an audiology assessment.*

Comments and Thoughts

One of the reasons I was immediately drawn to Tan's work was because she is willing to describe the language processing difficulty as a "delay" and **help** children and families deal with it early. So often it seems like we don't get special help for a child unless the problem is diagnosed as a disorder. A child with AP problems usually is not diagnosed as having the disorder until the age of eight or nine. It is true that as children mature, usually their ability to process language correctly improves. However, helping the child early may be a significant factor in improving communication and decreasing stress for everyone involved.

Subjects Dear To My Heart

I might have been an example of a child who talked well, but had listening difficulties. I remember my second-grade teacher thought there was something wrong and she sent me for a hearing test. I passed the test and was considered okay, I guess. But I talked too much and often when I should have been listening to the teacher. Tan mentions that some children may talk a lot because they understand better what they themselves are saying and that gives them a sense of control. I don't know. I wonder if that is why my father used to ask me to explain to him in my own words what he had just discussed with me. Maybe he was aware of my difficulties.

As a teacher and parent, I believe if I had known of the principle of using less words and speaking slowly I would have been of greater help to children who might have had delayed Audio Processing capabilities.

LEARNING BEFORE READING AND WRITING
with thanks to **WALTER ONG**

In the summer of 1997 when we were returning from a boat trip in British Columbia, Canada, I went ashore in Nanaimo to look around in the secondhand book stores. Scanning the shelves, I picked up a small paperback book, **Orality and Literacy by Walter Ong**. I opened it to no place in particular and I read several paragraphs. I wanted to read more so I bought it for $2.98!

This book has been a great treasure to me and of inestimable worth. Although I had studied Social Anthropology and had some understandings about the life world of people who had no reading or writing, Ong has given me an expanded view of that world and the importance of their ways of passing on knowledge. Ong emphasizes that speech is a basic, intrinsic characteristic of human beings. It is natural to us. Writing and reading are inventions of man and they have been developed in only a small proportion of all the known cultures of man (Ong, p.7).

The meaning and importance of speech (Ong, pp. 32, 33) is different in a primary oral culture from its perceived characteristics in our own "writing and reading" culture. Ong emphasizes that in a primarily oral culture, spoken words are important events and happenings; words are not thought of as "things" or as something that can be erased or changed. Words have power and they matter in special and intrinsic ways that are different from what we have become accustomed to thinking about them in a culture with strong emphasis on reading and writing.

Learning in an oral culture (Ong, pp. 33-51) is aided and abetted by such things as: hand and body movements that accompany a learning situation; observation, practice, and minimal verbal explanation at times; use of repetition, redundancy, rhythm, pattern, in singing, speaking, dancing, saying proverbs, etc. Active group participation is also important. The use of strong contrasts such as "the big bad wolf versus the cute little pigs" aids memory. Speaking of concrete things rather than abstract is important. Using lots of "ands" (being additive) rather than using subordinate clauses is also typical.

For learning more about Ong's ideas and research, I recommend studying *Orality and Literacy*. It is available over the Internet in sites such as ABE Books. See publishing data in the Bibliography.

Comments

One exciting result for me of discovering Ong's work was my feeling that all of this probably has bearing on the type of teaching methods that would be very effective for young children. To me it seems evident that the life and learning world of young children corresponds closely and naturally to the world of a people in a primary oral culture. I think of how children are often scared by just a word and also how just the right words or songs can provide a change of pace and comfort—yes, words of adults and other children are powerful and important to young children. A reasoned explanation to children cannot make up for the anger felt and expressed in their presence. The words of anger were/are an event, a happening, not words on a piece of paper to be torn up or quickly forgotten.

Since reading and writing have become the major "learning roads" in our culture and as adults we have worked hard to accomplish those skills, we probably have to some extent distanced ourselves from the traditional ways of learning that were and still are effective before "reading and writing." These old ways of teaching and learning may not come naturally and easily to us. They may even seem silly with all the repetition and need for hand and body movement, etc. We may be waiting for our children to grow up so that they can learn with reading and writing rather than taking the time to teach what can well be learned and probably should be learned by ear and observation and practiced with speech and body movements.

In the *Core Knowledge Preschool* manual (p.42) there are suggestions to use hand and body gestures and participatory verbal sentences in the telling of the folk tales, nursery rhymes, poems, etc. I was reviewing this book several years after I had read Ong's work. As a result of the information from both sources, I began to consciously make an effort to do this in my story telling sessions with kindergarten children. I found it very successful and the children loved it! I think as an "oral person" I have always done that to some extent, but doing it more so and consciously was an improvement.

Let's teach our children songs, poems, rhymes, and sayings and let's repeat them often and use hand motions and body language. As a part of our human heritage we need to enjoy verbal expression, repetition, rhythm, and body movement and all the layers of meaning inherent therein.

ADJUSTING TO FORMAL SCHOOL

It will, in most cases, take a conscious effort on the children's part to make the **transition** to the formal school setting. Preparation does help, but no amount of preparation covers everything. There are still new adults, many new children, a new environment, and new expectations to deal with.

The fact that formal school is "discontinuous" in many ways from preschool and home life may be important in helping children recognize that this is a different situation and they need to be watchful and attentive. If the child has had the opportunity to learn to take in the "lay of the land" in various places and to adjust their own activities accordingly as suggested in the paper on "Contrasts" then his or her adjustment to school may be easier.

Having practiced some of the skills needed in formal school can help greatly also. But formal school may be overwhelming to the child who has not learned and practiced different behaviors for different places.

In my latter teaching years, near **the end** of the year, I would "play like" a teacher in kindergarten or first grade. I would work with a small group of children who would be going into that environment and teach them to follow specific directions with a piece of paper. For example: Fold your paper in half. Put it in front of you so it opens like a book. Write your name on the top of the page. Open up the paper. Draw a picture of yourself, etc.

I once had a parent in the 1960s who was upset that our lab kindergarten had not taught his child how to stand in line so that he would have known what that was all about. Instead he got into trouble the first week of formal school for not standing in line correctly. (See discussion in Part VI of this book.)

Many people have spoken out in recent years about what children should be learning at home, in preschool, and in the community before "school." Parents should check with their school systems about what they expect kindergarten children or first-grade children to know prior to entry in the school. The following paper is about an early educator who spoke and wrote on this topic many, many years ago. Of course, today schools must educate all of the children. I think they need to start where each child can be successful. It is a big challenge. We may have to reinvent "school" in order for all children to learn.

JOHN AMOS COMENIUS (1592-1670) AND HIS BOOK, *THE SCHOOL OF INFANCY*

Comenius was not only an educator, he was also the last bishop of the old church of the Moravian and Bohemian Brethren in Europe. His work in education concerned all of the educational issues from infancy through university. He tried to see education from the perspective of the student. He thought trying to force learning by punishment was wrong. His ideas were revolutionary for that time.

Comenius recognized that the child who will probably do

well in formal school is usually prepared well in the home and community before he enters school. His little text, *The School of Infancy*, was written as a handbook for mothers. It provided detailed information about what he believed the child should be learning in "the school of the mother" before he went to formal school, which he advised should not be before the age of six, (Comenius, p. 116).

Most of the things he discussed were to be taught and practiced over a period of time. Foundations would be laid in the daily life of the young child by the adults' explicit and general teaching and also by the attitudes and beliefs of the parents. By the time the child was ready for formal school, he would be well prepared. Below I have listed some of the things that he thought children should have learned by age six, (Comenius, *The School of Infancy*, pp. 70-74, 85-100). I have updated the wording to be easier to understand.

> *God made us, and He is aware of our lives and what we are doing.*
> *Parents and teachers should be respected and obeyed.*
> *Children should know how to speak in different situations.*
> *They should know and use good manners.*
> *They should know when it is necessary to be quiet.*
> *Children should have learned many hand-skills such as: cutting, tying, folding, etc.*
> *They should know many songs by memory.*
> *Children should know many stories and folk tales and be able to retell some of them.*

Some of the more specific things he thought children should know were:

> *Place of birth and where they live now.*
> *The names of common things in the environment.*
> *The approximate meaning of units of time such as a minute, an hour, a day, etc.*
> *Something about the winter, spring, summer, and fall, our four seasons.*
> *Quantities vary – three is more than two.*
> *How to count to 20.*

Sudie Doughton Mason

The difference in a joke and something serious.
How to stick to the subject when asked about something.
The difference in a question and a statement.

Comenius emphasized that parents need to be good examples for their children and they should manage their own emotions and act reasonably. They should learn what children are capable of understanding and doing at each stage of development. Parents need to remember to teach the child, and to try to help the child save face and not appear stupid. He also discussed the importance of the children's learning from their daily play with each other. He did, however, caution that children should play with other children who would not cause them "more harm than good," (Comenius, p.90).

He emphasized that children learn through activity and they need something to do. They should be busy … occupied in "drawing, carrying, constructing," etc. And among other advice, he said it was valuable for the adults at times to play with the children (Comenius, pp. 91-92).

Comments

In the early 1990s, when I was visiting Mother at the Moravian Retirement Home in Winston Salem, North Carolina, one of her friends, a retired educator, showed me a copy of a current magazine, which featured Comenius and his work. The retired educator seemed surprised that I did not know about Comenius. I read the magazine and proceeded to look for more information. I found several copies of *The School of Infancy* in a store in the old Moravian village in Salem. The book was fascinating and I could see that many of our modern expectations had a long history.

I think it is interesting that there are many things mentioned here that are still important in preschool education, such as the stories and songs. But the emphasis of Comenius is on the child's learning and remembering them, not just having them presented. Also, it was not long ago that I saw a list of things children should be able to do before first grade, and counting to twenty was one of them!

In my collection of primers and readers from one hundred years ago, there is a lot of information about the seasons, about the life in school and home, and the common elements of it. There is also the practice of reading statements and answering questions. All those things remind me of Comenius.

Comenius mentioned many specific things which Montessori, approximately three hundred years later, made into neat little lessons, such as: cutting, folding, tying, rolling, unrolling, etc. Also he mentioned knowing how to keep silence, something a little different from just being quiet. That was also something Montessori wanted to teach the children. There are other interesting comparisons such as the importance of keeping your expectations in line with what the child could be successful at, and not making the child appear foolish, etc.

One of the things that Comenius believed was that education should not be forced, and he spoke out against the harshness of his times as mentioned earlier. Today we do not have much "harshness" and yet with warm schools, kind teachers, little fear of punishment, lots of materials and equipment, many children still do not succeed in school. Comenius was probably "right on" in emphasizing the connection between what a child had learned before school and his likely success in school.

It may be that schools are still expecting that most children will arrive at their doors with specific knowledge and attitudes. Often there is a list handed out to parents and preschool teachers about what the child should know before school. I have also noticed that many school districts now have important Early Childhood programs for three- and four-year-olds that work with the community and the parents to increase the numbers of children who arrive for kindergarten and first grade well prepared.

It is interesting today that most people seem to think education is important, but many people do not think religion is very important or necessary for a meaningful and good life. Comenius believed that faith and moral education were the foundations for life and needed to come before and continue while learning arts and literature and science. He spoke in depth to his concerns for the spiritual and moral education of children in *The School of Infancy*.

Today we have great expectations and the hope that all people in a democratic society will have the opportunity to find personal meaning and fulfillment in their work and lives. Education is seen as the major factor in making that a possibility. Most educators are aware today that many children have not learned the attitudes and concepts that foster a quick adjustment and success in regular school. We must remember these children are not stupid. Many of them are bright and capable and they have already learned many things to help them survive in their immediate home and community situations. But as far as formal school goes, they are like foreigners arriving on a new planet. I wonder what advice Comenius would give us if he were alive today.

"IT'S MINE" – IMPORTANCE OF OWNERSHIP AND RELATIONSHIP

On reflection it seems to me that knowing something is **ours,** is connected to us in a strong bond, and knowing and **feeling responsible for our part in the situation** is crucial in our development. For some people, an intense feeling that something is theirs may come early and last long, for others it may happen with a crisis experience like it did for Jacob in his feelings about God, (Genesis 28: 16-22). Jacob, of course, had known about God—the God of his forefathers, Abraham and Isaac, but now he accepted this God as **"mine**," (re: verse 21, "...then the Lord shall be **my** God."). And he went so far in recognizing responsibility in the relationship that he vowed to give ten percent of what the Lord gave him as stated in verse 22 of Genesis, chapter 28.

It was the Rev. Fred Hertzog who made this experience of Jacob's become very meaningful to me while we were team teaching a Sunday school class for seventh-graders fifteen or twenty years ago. With some intensity and passion he explained to the students what these verses had meant to him in his life; how as a young person after studying Jacob's experience he, Fred, had wrestled with what God meant to him personally. He decided that, Yes, God was his God in a special personal way. No longer was he just some generic God that created everything and looked after the world in general!

A foundation for faith had been laid for both Jacob and my friend Fred, but it took some specific experiences and struggle before either of them felt a strong personal connection with God.

I believe that the sense of something being "ours" may come about over a long period of time or may come about in a sudden awakening, but in both instances it is the **inner response** of the person to accept what is offered that clinches the deal.

Jean-Henri Fabre, as described in *The Passionate Observer*, was fascinated by insects as a young child. He never lost this interest or quit observing even when others laughed at him. He never stopped going to the field to observe and study the insects even though he had to complete studies in something else in order to make a living early in his life. He always knew that insects were his true passion; eventually, others recognized his knowledge and he was able to work in his chosen area of interest.

My father remembered fixing the hole in the bucket used for drawing water from the well. He took a rock and beat on the little hole until the metal came together. He had watched his big brothers working metal in their shop and he had observed that metal could change. All his life he liked to work on problems and he knew he could "fix things. This was an ability that was "his."

I believe when we have some basic knowledge about some subject and then we are presented with something new to do or understand, we must concentrate and make a little jump for it. We are right on what I call our "learning edge." Aha, I did it. I understand. I believe. I think. I wonder. I observe. I remember. I am aware. This is **mine** now. It is not just the adult's knowledge, not just my big brother's knowledge, not just the smart kids', it is mine.

I used to tell children in my final teaching years that one of the good things about learning something was that then it became "yours" in a sense. It was a story you knew, it was a tree you could identify, it was a skill you had mastered, it was a poem that you loved, it was a song you could sing. Wow!

"This is my family." "This is my house." "This is my school." "These are my friends." Suddenly I am reminded of the topics Betty chose for the children to draw for the yearbooks, (see paper on Year Book project in the Montessori section, Part VI). Those topics may have been important in both a direct and indirect way in helping children understand and appreciate some of the things that were theirs.

I believe that when children go through the early stage of

"**Me and Mine**" it is so important to help children see that, yes, this is yours. By letting children protect their own things and not always have to share, they hopefully learn to accept that others have things they want to protect and they may not always share. It is important for children to go through this stage and for adults to understand its value.

The ability to share "what is mine" in appropriate ways usually develops over time. Having our own needs met and learning to recognize the needs and interests of others as we grow helps lay a foundation for the willingness to share. Also having good experiences working and playing with others helps us understand that sometimes in sharing we have more than in keeping everything to ourselves. For example, when I share my ball with someone else, there are many games we can play that I cannot play alone. This could be the subject of another paper!

I do have to laugh a little about this, because it is like so many things in life. We have to be vigilant; sharing may bring problems. My father told me that when he was about five he let a lot of friends look at his collection of baseball cards and it wasn't long before he noticed some were missing. So he learned to check what was there and recheck when they were handed back! Being generous and sharing does not mean we should let others take advantage of us.

Thinking back to the paper on Comenius and my comments about children who have problems adjusting and learning in school, I wonder if part of the difficulty is that those children never feel that this is truly **their school, their business, their responsibility.**

Comments

Of course as we become mature adults, we gain new meanings and let go of old ideas about relationship and ownership. We don't own other people. Yet if parents do not bond with an infant and feel this child is mine and my responsibility they may lack the passion and will to sacrifice as needed for the child's welfare or even the ability to continue caring and interacting with the child at difficult times.

As the child is growing up, the way in which the parents care and take responsibility will change. Children learn gradually to be more and more independent and responsible for themselves in many settings, and adults are responsible for monitoring that growth in some ways. The nature of the relationship changes and it has to change for everyone to move forward.

INDIVIDUAL DIFFERENCES

Most parents and teachers are well aware of individual differences: differences in learning styles, differences in ability, differences in visual and auditory perception, differences in physical appearance, differences in motivation, and differences in foundational knowledge and on and on the list goes. We have heard a lot about individual differences in recent years.

I don't believe that most preschool age children like to focus on their differences. In general they seem to feel comfortable in being "like" others. They seem to enjoy games together like "London Bridge," "Drop the Handkerchief," "Duck, duck, Goose," etc. Songs like "Head, Shoulders, Knees, and Toes" involve every child touching the same body part and in essence emphasizing our sameness. Of all the games I played with little children, the one they loved the most was done with partners. Touch knees to knees, forehead to forehead, elbows to elbows. Now move to a new partner. I would say a few different moves with each partner. Our favorite paired exercise was the "wash through" (turning under with hands held). By the end all children had been a partner with every other child in the group.

I once heard a speaker at a conference for Head Start teachers say that if you only had one child from a certain minority group, do not have a study on "his" group. He thought it was very upsetting to the child to be pointed out as different from everyone else.

It is natural, however, that during the preschool years both the adults and children begin to notice differences. One child is a better climber, another draws well, another is a big talker, one shows a talent for music. Often children have difficulty accepting the situation when they first see peers who can do things much better than they can. Sometimes parents are upset about this too. This may become a moment of growth and new understandings as parents or teachers discuss this situation with children.

It is not so much the facts of the matter as it is how we

interpret it and how we decide to act. Yes, we are all different in some ways and alike in some ways. It's okay. Further discussion may be needed from time to time. Observation of your child and listening to his or her comments may cue you as to the need to talk further or the need to spend time helping your child gain the desired abilities. Possibly you need to look for different teaching and learning methods. Positive remarks may help, such as, "With practice you'll be able to throw the ball better." Reading books to children that speak to this topic of differences in talents and learning abilities may also help.

Mentioning to children when they are four or five that there are different ways of learning and knowing may give some support to the children for what they have already observed. Some of us have to study piece by piece and proceed in a careful and sequential way while others just seem to absorb some types of knowledge in a haphazard way and some people do seem born with unusual innate abilities. And it may be that people need to use different ways of learning for different kinds of material. I believe that there were times I thought I could not learn something and that assumption was based on the fact that I did not learn it easily by the method in which it was being taught to me.

My father had told me when I was a child and I complained about not being as smart as a lot of children in my class that it was okay for me to be me. He said that if I did the best I could that he was sure my life would be fine. He also told me that he had known a lot of talented and smart people and that those people did not necessarily have a better all-around life than more average folks. I never said that in those words to my preschoolers but I think knowing that helped me to not be too focused on high achievement for its own sake.

I would caution against making light of the accomplishments of others or putting too much emphasis on them. Again, being continually interested in your child and his or her progress and having a belief in your child's ability to learn and overcome problems is very important. And we need to value and care about our children just as they are every day and not make our broad love or acceptance of them dependent on their early success in music or sports or academics or whatever. Just being, trying, and practicing and experimenting are all valuable and should be appreciated by parents. But at the same time it is the parents' responsibility to monitor the child's growth and development and to seek help if the child needs it.

I liked our multi-age Montessori classroom where the children learned to show enthusiasm and interest in what other children were doing even though it was quite different from what they were working on. With a little encouragement from us teachers, I found the older children were smiling and showing interest at the efforts and accomplishments of the younger children. The threes and fours seemed to naturally show interest and awe in the accomplishments of the older children.

Maybe parents could help siblings get along better by helping the children appreciate the particular interests and developing skills of each person in the family. The older child may specifically need help in valuing what the younger child is doing. We should not underestimate the influence of other children on a child's attitudes and progress.

Remember what we are feeling and thinking may be communicated in subtle ways to the child even if we don't speak it out loud. So when we are upset, rather than thinking or saying, "How stupid," or "How troublesome you are," or "Why aren't you like your big sister?"...think about accepting and loving this child, and say something that will help the child and you work in a positive way in the situation.

Often one of the reasons we adults may react so negatively when our child is having problems is because people may have treated us that way in similar situations in our own childhood. But we do not have to act that way. We can practice becoming more objective and low-key in a situation where our child is having difficulty. A calm attitude may help the child learn and progress better than our being upset. But denying any problem is not a help.

Certainly just being low-key and not upset will not solve all the problems in life. There may be times when a different approach is needed. We have to come up with ways to practice and learn and find little aids to help ourselves and the children we work with. We need to remember our individual differences. We have to help children discover coping styles and ways of learning that work for them. Hopefully all the new brain research will be able to help us in this endeavor.

HANDMADE MATERIALS

Handmade materials and activities have a special quality. This has seemed evident to me since my childhood. My grandmother had made me a quilt which I still have today. My father made me a dollhouse, and my mother made interesting clothes for my first doll. Some things were made in response to a request from one of us children, such as the clod-wooden sandals that would make a lot of noise and annoy the two "old-maid" neighbors. Of course we did not tell Dad why we wanted them.

Today we live in such a commercial society and everything has a price and most things can be replaced. It seems refreshing to think of people making some unique things for themselves and others. I have a dear friend who has made blankets for my grandson's babies. She embroiders each child's name on their blankets. These handmade blankets speak to the child and family over and over that someone cared enough to spend time and effort to make something special for them. Their value is on a higher level than money.

In my graduate education and in my first teaching jobs (1960-1982), although I had made a few things with the children or for them, I do not remember reading of its value or attending workshops or lectures about it. When I studied Montessori's writings midway in my career, circa 1983, I found that she mentioned that it was important for the teacher to make some of the materials if possible. Betty had made her pink tower, brown stair, long rods, tactile numbers and letters, button frame, lacing frame, and many other things.

I made many materials also. My husband helped greatly with his woodworking skills and creative abilities. He made wonderful wooden boxes to hold things, a board with many varied doors with different types of latches and locks, a set with small to large bolts and nuts. The children seemed to show special interest in the fact that we had made these things ourselves. Sometimes they wanted us to tell how we had made them. Children today have very few opportunities to see things made from start to finish.

There is much to ponder here. If an adult has made something for a child's use, how is it different from the child having a similar bought item? I remember my mother commenting that as a teenager she felt embarrassed about the old handmade quilts and coverlets at her home, and she thought the new, store-bought things would be so much nicer! And I don't think my husband was so happy with his homemade underwear when he went to school, even though it was beautifully hand-sewn by his mother just for him. So the prevailing ideas of our peers and culture will also affect how we value things.

Maybe in the old days most of what people had was handmade. That might have made homemade things not seem so unusual or important. In some instances people may have objected to the amount of time and energy it took to produce them. I remember my maternal grandmother's diaries in which she complained about all the time and hard work that went into sewing clothes for everyone in the family. There was probably a great sense of relief in the first generation of people in our country who did not have to make so many things!

For me, handmade things were not usually the items we had to have, but rather they were something extra, like the clogs or sled mentioned earlier. As a child I remember going to the creek not far from our house and digging out the clay to make camels, sheep, and stands for the clothespin dolls that Mother fashioned for our family crèche. I remember sensing that my mother enjoyed doing this. It was important and fun to her to make things by hand. This little nativity scene became a part of our Christmas traditions. We put it up on the mantel each Christmas season. Mother had even figured out a way for the camels to stand using popsicle sticks. Years later I made a set with our children. My elder daughter has made a set with her children. Each set is a little different. Powerful memories and unspoken emotions reside for us with those handmade crèches!

MY FAVORITE BOOKS FOR YOUNG CHILDREN

- *Ask Mr. Bear.* Marjorie Flack. New York: Macmillan, 1958.
- *Blueberries for Sal.* Robert McCloskey. New York: The Viking

Press, 1948.
- *Crictor.* Tomi Ungerer. New York: Harper and Row, Publishers, 1958.
- *Caps for Sale.* Sloboodkina, Esphyr. New York: Walter Scott, Inc., 1940.
- *Cactus Hotel.* Brenda Z. Guiberson. New York: Henry Holt and Company, 1991.
- *Chicken Little Count to Ten.* Margaret Frisky and Katherine Evans. Chicago: Childrens Press, 1946.
- *The Christmas Whale.* Roger Duvoisin. New York: Alfred A. Knopf, 1943.
- *Crow Boy.* * Taro Yashima. New York: The Viking Press, 1955.
- *Don't Cry Big Bird.* Sarah Roberts. New York: Random House, 1981.
- *Eric Carle's Dragons, Dragons and other Creatures that Never Were.* * Compiled by Laura Whipple. New York: Philomel Books, 1991.
- *A Gift Bear for the King.* Carl Memling. New York: E.P. Dutton and Co., 1966.
- *The Golden Egg Book.* Margaret Wise Brown. Illustrated by Leonard Weisgard. A Golden Book. Racine: Western Publishing Company, 1947.
- *The Golden Egg Book.* Margaret Wise Brown. Illustrated by Lillian Obligado. Racine: Western Pub. Co., 1962.
- *Gordon and the Glockenspiel.* Lee Ryland. Racine, Wisconsin: Whitman Publishing Company, 1966.
- *How my Parents Learned to Eat.* Ina Friedman. Boston: Houghton Mifflin, 1984.
- *Jacko.* John Goodall. New York: Harcourt Brace Jovanovich, 1972.
- *Little One-Inch and other Japanese Children's Favorite Stories.* * Edited by Florence Sakade. Tokyo, Japan and Rutland, Vermont: Charles E. Tuttle Co., Inc., 1958. 13th printing, 1990.
- *Many Moons.* * James Thurber. New York: Harcourt, Brace and Company, 1943.
- *Mikosch.* Thomas and Wanda Zacharias (a story in German which I had a friend translate for me when I lived in Chile)

Subjects Dear To My Heart

- *Millions of Cats.* Wanda Gag. New York: Coward-McCann, Inc., 1928.
- *The Monkey and the Crocodile.* Paul Galdone. New York: The Seabury Press, 1969.
- *My Painted House, My Friendly Chicken and Me.* Maya Angelou. New York: Clarkson Potter, Inc., 1994.
- *Ola.** Ingri and Edgar Parin d'Aulaire. New York: Doubleday, Doran and Co., 1932.
- *Paddle to the Sea.** Holling Clancy Holling Boston: Houghton Mifflin Co., 1941.
- *A Pair of Red Clogs.* Masako Matsuno. Cleveland: The World Publishing Company, 1960.
- *Peter and the Wolf.** Sergei Prokofiev. Many books are available. I've misplaced my copy which I liked with its stylized illustrations and a picture of the instrument being played with a line from the music when each character was introduced.
- *Runaway Bunny.* Margaret Wise Brown. Scranton, Pa.: HarperCollins Children's Books, 1972.
- *Rechenka's Eggs.* Patricia Polacco. New York: Philomel Books, 1988.
- *The Sailor Dog.* Margaret Wise Brown. A Golden Book, New York. Racine: Western Publishing Co., 1953.
- *Sea Bird.** Holling Clancy Holling. Boston: Houghton Mifflin Company, 1948.
- *Stories for Children**. Lev Tolstoi. English translation. Moscow: Progress Publishers, 1991.
- *The Story about Ping.* Marjorie Flack and Kurt Wiese. New York: Viking Press, 1933.
- *The Three Pigs.* Illustrated by Barbara Pritzen. Racine: Golden Press, Western Publishing Co., 1973.
- *Ten Small Tales.* Celia Barker Lottridge. Toronto: A Groundwood Book, Douglas and McIntyre Ltd., 1993.
- *Up a Tree.* By Winifred and Cecil Lubell. Eau Claire, Wisconsin: E.M. Hale and Co., 1964.
- *Where the Wild Things Are.* Maurice Sendak. New York: Harper and Row, 1963.

* These books are longer or have more complicated stories than the others. Usually I used them with children who were at least five years old.

Comments

Over the forty years of my career, I have read many lists of books for children and I am always surprised to find that a few of my favorites are not included. But I have noticed that many of the same books do occur in list after list. Fortunately, there is an abundance of good books for young children. I like many of the classics the best because they have stood the test of time and continue to be liked by a lot of children and adults. Books such as *Millions of Cats, Runaway Bunny,* and many versions of *The Three Little Pigs* and *The Three Bears* fit in the classic category. I think all children can identify with the plots and the characters.

I am always overjoyed to find some lovely, maybe old, but "new to me" children's book such as *Flight of the Animals* by Claudine or *The Secret Hiding Place* by Rainey Bennett. Both of these I just discovered in the past several months. One was at a church bazaar and the other in an antique store! In both books, the illustrations and story are delightful. I have had good luck finding copies of out-of-print children's books on Web sites for used books.

The first list I made of Suggested Books for Young Children was made at the request of a Head Start regional director over thirty years ago. I now have many other books that I have added to my list and probably some I deleted from the original list.

It is a good idea for adults to read first or at least look over any book they plan to read to a child or group of children to be sure it is appropriate for their age and development. However, I have not always been right about what a child would like or understand. Many books can be enjoyed in a small group or with one adult reading to one child that might not be suitable for a large group story time or even reading to several children of different ages. On the other hand, some children probably begin to like a book because the teacher and the other children are enthusiastic about it.

Remember, children love to hear the same story over and over. Also, there are many ways to extend the use of any one book. Each time you read it again you may think of one new thing about the story or ask the children if they noticed anything they had not been aware of before. Learning about the artist and the way the illustrations were made or discussing why the particular type of illustration is good for this particular story may be interesting to some children. Other suggestions are included in the paper "Story Time – Outline of a Workshop," which immediately follows this paper.

STORY TIME – OUTLINE OF A WORKSHOP

I. The purpose of story time
    A. Shared delight
    B. Provide general knowledge
    C. Provide a base of traditional stories that helps to give the children common experience that is shared with peers and with adults.
    D. Help children learn to listen to the leader and develop group participation skills
    E. Help develop vocabulary and language skills
    F. Concomitant uses of story time
        1. Learning the difference in imaginary stories and realistic stories
        2. Experience the same story in different formats
        3. Learning something about the culture of print and different types of illustrations.

II. Prerequisites to a successful story time with a group of children
    A. Use of transition activities - finger plays, songs, and other routine ways of calming down and focusing for that particular group
    B. Children are seated so that each can see the teacher and illustrations in the book if that method is being used.
    C. Distractions are at a minimum.
    D. Children who have trouble attending are sitting close to the adult and not near other children who might bother them.
    E. Books or stories and methods of presentation are chosen with the age and abilities and interests of the

children in mind.
- F. Consider your own feelings about a book before you read it to a group. Children tend to pick up our underlying feelings about things. I once heard a great storyteller tell a story I had always disliked, but in his telling I found it charming. I have also found that sometimes if the children liked a book, I tended to grow fond of it too.

III. Various story reading and telling methods and techniques
- A. Reading the book as written – showing the pictures as you read. Many of the classic books for young children are best presented in this way. Examples: *Blueberries for Sal, Ping, Caps for Sale, Millions of Cats,* etc.
- B. Telling the story using a flannel board and flannel-backed characters. Old nursery tales such as *The Three Little Pigs, The Three Bears, The Gingerbread Man,* etc. work well in this medium. Also the story can be elaborated on or shortened as need be.
- C. Using puppets – The teacher uses the puppets while telling the story. This is also a good medium for the old tales.
- D. Letting the children use the puppets – Use a story that the children know well. Learning how to hold the puppets and saying your part might best be done in a group of four or five children where each person has a puppet. Or the children could be divided into several groups with one group being the audience and the other group the actors. Then switch so that all the children have a chance to participate. The children enjoy the repetition.
- E. Having the children act out a well-known story such as *The Three Bears.*
- F. Having audio tapes available so that children can look at a book and listen with earphones during activity time. Many sets of books with tapes are commercially available or in your public library. In the tapes, the speaker usually pauses and rings a bell for the child to turn a page. If you make your own tapes try to include the pause and bell for the turning of the pages.

Subjects Dear To My Heart

    G. Read a story and show the picture after you have read a page. This is a good challenge after children have mastered listening to stories while you show the picture.

    H. Tell a story with no pictures. You can watch the children's faces as you tell the story. This is a time-honored method and a good one for the children to use their own imaginations.

IV. Further Ideas

    A. Make up your own "Must Read or Tell List" of books and stories and use it from year to year.

    B. Collect props that can be used over and over…like a cap collection for acting out *Caps for Sale.*

    C. Help children remember titles, main characters, plots, etc.

        1. Read or tell the name of the book or story before reading or telling it. Emphasize it by saying something like: The title of this book is____. After the story you can ask who remembers the title of the story. Give a hint if needed.

        2. Have a "Do You Remember Moment" now and then.

            a. Repeat the words of some character in a recently read or told story and ask who said that. Choose easy to remember characters at first, such as, "Oh no, someone sat in my chair and broke it all to pieces!" After someone tells the character, ask if anyone remembers the title of the story.

            b. Act out a motion from a recent story such as The *Three Little Pigs.* Example: blow fiercely and put your fingers up for cars. Of course the answer is the bad wolf. Then check to see if anyone remembers the title of that story, etc.

            c. The teacher can wear something similar to a character in a story and ask, "Who am I portraying?" Examples: a bunch of caps stacked up on the teacher's head for the peddler in *Caps for Sale*, a large yellow rain hat to portray Scuppers from *Scuppers the Sailor Dog*, etc.

    d. Eventually some of the children may want a turn at acting out a part and having everyone guess who it is.

D. Observe for growth and changes during the year, e.g., children's interest in longer stories at the end of the year and/or the ability of a child to retell a story in his/her own words.

E. Remember that children love repetition and they will enjoy hearing the same story over and over. They may begin to know it by memory and they can say it with you as you read. They may also have new ideas and questions about the story or illustrations as they review the story from time to time.

ASKING QUESTIONS

I have noticed that the primers and first readers of a century ago usually included questions after one or two pages of reading. Most of these readers were teaching basic information as well as reading. For example a first reader might start out with a few sentences about the fall season and what happens in fall. Then there would be questions. I believe that because the reading was about something the child already knew a little about, it was easier to read and also easier to remember what the book had said. I also think the questions helped the child to remind himself of the material he had read. In many instances the child could go back and check it if he didn't know the answer.

After looking over the old readers with all the questions, I decided to ask the children in my class a few questions after I read a story at group time. I had done this before on occasion, but had never systematically done it or thought much about it. After doing it frequently and remembering to pay attention to this, I found out that many times the children did not understand something or remember something that I had thought they would have. And they did not seem to automatically remember to remember. They needed to be reminded to remember and to practice it just as we would any other skill. So I began to ask them more questions every day not just at story time. I asked questions while we were standing in line to go to the wash room, or when we were gathering for a group time and were waiting for all the children to arrive. It became a game for us.

I was sorry it took me so many years to catch on to asking children questions, because the children seemed to learn a lot and remember much better after I began the daily questions. Before asking a question I might clue the children that one was forthcoming. "Put on your thinking cap," I'd frequently say. I tried to ask each child a question that I thought he or she could answer easily—especially in the beginning to help build confidence. I tried to relate the questions to something the child had done recently or something we had discussed in group time the day before.

I found that I liked asking each child a question rather than throwing out the question and having the children raise their hands. If I didn't have time to ask everyone, I'd choose three children to ask questions to now and three more later and a different three the next time, etc. It meant I had to remember who had been asked. But the children caught on quickly and would remind me of who needed a turn. I also had times when the group could answer a question in unison. That was especially fun with addition facts and rhyming words.

After the children were familiar with questions and answers, I might let them tell me a topic they wanted their question to be about; e.g., dinosaurs, math, birds, rhyming words, etc. Sometimes I'd give them a topic to ask me a question about.

The children improved in their confidence in speaking in front of the group and in waiting to answer until they were called upon. Usually I said the name of the child whose turn it was before I asked the question. This seemed to help others not to give out the answer. I explained that part of the game was keeping the answers in your mind only…unless it was your turn. The children learned to listen to each other and never to laugh at anyone's answer.

By choosing questions that I thought the child would have a good chance of knowing, there weren't many wrong answers. If there was a wrong answer, it was okay. I might say, "good try" or I might give the child a hint and let him try again if he wanted to.

Usually with the hint he would get it. I did not ask another child the missed question. This was a way to help the children "save face" as at three and four children are just learning about this; I did not want them to feel discouraged. Of course, competent children at five and six can handle being "not right" all the time, essentially because they are right most of the time. But children of any age may need a little help "saving face." I tried to remember the things each child had not understood. At a later time, we could provide activities and lessons to help.

As with many things that turn out to be good learning tools for children, this turned out better than I could have ever guessed. I have read somewhere that it is also important to ask children questions that do not have one exact specific right answer, but that stimulate thought or give the child a chance to state an opinion. This reminds me somewhat of the difference in skills and creativity or in convergent and divergent thinking. In life we will need it all.

I have noticed with children I have tutored that they often do not have a good sense of what sort of questions need a specific answer and what sort of questions are just to give a general answer about. By using a prefix to a question such as "What do you think about....?" may cue the child that this is a thought or opinion question. If we want them to tell us the answer to 2 plus 2 it could be stated simply, "What is 2 plus 2?" One child I was tutoring for math who was in sixth grade did not know the multiplication tables by heart and when I suggested that that might be one of the problems, he countered with, "Well, I know most of them most of the time and if I don't know an answer exactly, well, I will be pretty close." This seemed sufficient and reasonable to this child probably because that was a model that worked in some situations.

EDUCATIONAL STRATEGIES I OBSERVED IN VARIOUS MONTESSORI SCHOOLS

These are strategies which I think could be used in many different settings with young children. Most of these are also discussed in Montessori's own books, which are listed in the Bibliography.
- The use of relatively quiet voices in the room during the major activity and work time.
- Keeping distractions at a minimum. Walls are usually a fairly light and unobtrusive color. Pictures and posters on the walls are minimal. Children are taught to walk quietly.
- Adults were spending some time observing children.
- Having materials that will interest the child and promote his/her learning to concentrate.
- The use of slow motions when showing very young children how to do something, e.g., threading a bead, washing hands, outlining a shape, buttoning, pouring, etc.
- Speaking as little as possible when you are demonstrating an activity. If you talk too much, the young child's attention may be attracted to your face and voice and not to the movements of your hands while doing the activity.
- Simplifying and removing unnecessary differences. For instance, when teaching shapes all the shapes are the same color and a similar size so that the child's attention is drawn to the differences in form.
- Helping the child think through each part of an activity: preparation, doing to completion, put away.
- Providing some relatively easy activities. These seemed to help the child to build confidence and mastery and they did not require much attention from the teacher.
- Using the Skills the child has mastered to provide a basis for new and more complex and challenging activities.
- Encouraging the children without overdoing the praise. Notice the child's own satisfaction that naturally comes with doing and completing an activity. Beware of making the children dependent on adult praise or some physical reward.
- Backing up to where the child can be successful ...if he/she is having a problem.

- Using some handmade materials. Showing or talking about how they were made helps the child see a sequence in the making process. They are also evidence that not everything must be "bought."
- Providing some beautiful and well-made educational items that are satisfying to the eye and hand. Often today children are only given plastic things which do not require much care on their part and also do not help the child to appreciate a wide variety of textures.
- Treating broken items as a "sad event" and removing them from the room for a while. If possible the children may be able to help with the repair. And the group can be prepared for the return of the item to the classroom and for its proper care.
- Providing large blocks of time in which the child may choose which educational activities to use. This promotes the development of initiative, gives a child a chance to do easy, somewhat more difficult, and challenging activities, all according to his own work cycle.

ESPECIALLY FOR TEACHERS

THE FACE OF THE TEACHER

- The default look or "face" of the preschool and primary teacher should reflect purposefulness, calmness, warmth, and interest in each child.
- The teacher must be fair and teach and be with all children. By maintaining a calm facial expression, other children may see the teacher as fair and interested in everyone. Lots of praise and "cheerful" attention to the high achievers or "good" children sets up the idea that some kids are teacher's pets. This may interfere with relationships among the children as well as have other bad outcomes.
- With a generally even disposition, the teacher can change facial expressions slightly to show varying amounts of pleasure or displeasure. A person who starts out from an overly cheerful attitude does not have much room to show pleasure without

getting giddy or overdoing the praise. A person who starts from a general grouchy look may have to become very upset before people notice.
- If the teacher shows interest, approval, dislike of certain behaviors, etc. in small ways, the child may be less overwhelmed by the adult's attention, praise, and their own mistakes and better able to concentrate on the learning for its own sake.
- Children for one reason or another may not want adult attention on them personally and they might withdraw efforts in certain activities if the response from the adults is gushy and makes them feel singled out or set up for some superior future achievement.
- A "too friendly" teacher may inadvertently give the child the idea that backstage behavior is permissible. Backstage behavior is very informal behavior that may be acceptable around the family or very close friends.
- Also, a "too friendly" teacher may be looking for the children to meet her/his emotional needs.
- Beginning any new relationship on a rather neutral tone may be a good idea. I remember when a friend moved into a retirement home, someone advised her not to be too friendly to everyone in the beginning. "Some folks will grab hold of anyone who is friendly and you'll have trouble moving backwards to a more uninvolved relationship."
- I have noticed that most young children want space between themselves and a new teacher. They may feel threatened by the adult's attempt to be too friendly toward them. Respecting the child and giving each one time to warm up to a new teacher is important.
- Some children live in hyper emotional environments. They may have learned to fear the emotional reactions of the adults. They are on guard so to speak and it is hard for them to focus on learning because they are watching everything going on around them in order to protect themselves. It may take a while for the child to adjust to less intense adults and to learn to trust. These children may have to be taught what the teacher's facial expressions mean in a rather explicit way.
- Balance is the key. If the teacher is overly controlling of her own emotions, she may seem stiff, unreal, or unapproachable.

This is really a big subject that deserves careful consideration. Often adults are not aware of their own "face," so to speak. I was shocked one time when someone told me that I at times laughed inappropriately. On close observation of myself I determined that this was in fact true and I indeed might be sending meanings to others that I had not intended.

Note:

All of my elementary school teachers seemed to me to be good teachers in that they were concerned with helping children learn and they were focused on that. Most of those teachers were "old maids" dedicated to teaching children, and their dedication was evident even when as children we were upset about something they did or said. They were all at least forty years old and many may have been in their fifties or sixties! Those teachers were rather **formal yet somewhat warm** at the same time. Sometimes I thought they cared more about the kids that acted eager to learn or the ones who were real smart. One thing was for sure, they did not put up with bad behavior. However, I never saw a teacher hit a child with a ruler or with her hand. I did see a few marched off to "the office."

My best teachers in junior high and high school were **not friendly and/or warm during class**. They seemed purposefully focused on getting to the subject matter as quickly as possible and helping the students learn and master the materials. The overly friendly teachers seemed too interfering and not appropriate to me as we kids were trying to enter adolescence and we really wanted "our space." None of the friendly, warm teachers in high school seemed to be as good at teaching the subject matter as the ones that were not that way. Students who did not seem to care about learning, however, did not seem to learn with the friendly, warm teacher or the "cooler" and focused ones. Maybe there is research about this. In college, my faculty advisors were warm in the "one on one" counseling sessions. In class they were cooler and treated everyone more formally.

It is important for all children to have parents and/or other significant adults in their lives who are warm and caring toward them and not distant and uninvolved in their total life. For one friend of mine who overcame a non-nurturing home environment, it was the school nurse who recognized her needs and guided and encouraged her in every way. For another friend it was her Sunday school teacher. For another it was her next door neighbor.

TEACHER AND PARENT RELATIONSHIPS

Looking back, I was not always as open and honest with parents about my concerns for their child as I might have been. I was not assertive with parents who already seemed to have made their minds up about many things. I think I tended to think everything would be okay because I usually felt confident about the parents' ability to raise their child and make appropriate judgment calls. I don't think I liked criticism myself and maybe I was afraid my comments would be interpreted that way. I do know that I am dogmatic and opinioned and maybe I was trying to avoid that with the parents.

In cases where I was a friend of the parents before the child had ever been in school, maybe the relationship was even more complex. Maybe some parents who were my friends feared sharing thoughts and questions with me. I don't think I was always consciously aware of this while I was still teaching. But I have thought about it in writing this book. Friendships often have been built on understanding and acceptance, common interests and points of view, and conviviality. Bad feelings might result from discussing a child's difficulties or other "hot" issues.

I remember hearing in my early teaching career back in the 1960s something that may have been connected with this. If there was a choice possible, it was better for the child to have a teacher that was not a good friend of the parent's. In my childhood, I remember that if a child was in the same school where their parent was a teacher, that child was placed in another teacher's room if possible. Is there a conflict with teaching/learning and emotional closeness? I think there might be with some people or in some circumstances.

I have wondered how to lessen the negative impact of this. Teachers and parents who are friends outside the classroom may find themselves face to face in the teacher/parent conference or at other times with concerns about the child. I think the important issue is to be sure that information or questions that either the parent or the teacher has that might be pertinent to the child's welfare be discussed. As a teacher or a parent, ask for another time to get together to continue the discussion if you feel the issues need further exploration. Having both parents attend and also another teacher may be helpful.

If some major decision is to be made, it may be best to bring up the options, but leave a day or two before the decision is finalized, so that all parties have time to think further on their own while they are not in the presence of each other. Either the teacher or the parent may too quickly agree with what the other proposes due to many reasons, some previously mentioned.

Part III
My Education to Become a Teacher

In memory of my mother,
    Janie Gold Caroline Gooch Doughton

    Mother always cared about all little children. She expressed her ideas and concerns for them frequently. She remembered a lot about growing up as an only child in the small North Carolina town of Stem. "Janie" enjoyed fishing in the creek, tramping to the woods for blackberries, and the other work/play activities that the next door neighbor, Mrs. Bullock, instigated and supervised to keep her children and Janie happily occupied. She also often visited with Mrs. Hall who lived near by. Mrs. Hall once told me that she asked Janie if she wanted to learn how to bake a cake. She had replied, "Oh, no, what I want to learn is how to bake potatoes!" So that day they dug up a few potatoes from the garden and baked them. Mother also loved being with Lassiter and Mary, the Hall's two young children. They remained lifelong friends.

    Mother became a dedicated first-grade teacher in the 1920s. She taught for ten years prior to her marriage. Many of those years were at the North Elementary in Winston Salem, North Carolina. She said she loved teaching so much she would have paid the school to let her teach! She taught every child she ever had how to read. One year she even had forty students who were in the low third of ability rating. She told me, "That year was especially hard and I almost lost my voice."

"I think I was a better teacher than a mother," she confided to me in her later years. We discussed it and decided that was probably natural to feel that way. After all, with raising your own children you are there for life. You are continually seeing the outcomes of things and wondering if you made the right decisions at times. Also teaching a child to read is a very focused goal and since that had been a major accomplishment of hers as a teacher she had something specific to feel successful about.

Mother always wanted to have a big family. She said she had originally wanted nine children, but since she got married kind of late she guessed four was fine! Our yard and home were open to all the neighborhood children. In 1944, during the polio epidemic in Charlotte, N.C., the children could not leave their neighborhoods. Mother proceeded to read stories to all the children on Vail Avenue who cared to come every afternoon at one-thirty!

Mother and Dad believed that every child should be at the table for any important family meal. If there was a baby, Dad probably held him or her. When the baby got bigger, he/she had a highchair that could be pulled up close to the table. And after the highchair, cushions were added to chairs so that a little child could eat and see everyone better.

At both of the Methodist churches that we had belonged to during my childhood, Mother taught the first grade Sunday school class. In both places we lived, she gave a neighborhood Christmas party where the children played out the Nativity story and the parents came to watch. The children were invited first to the refreshment table, in honor of the Christ child and his birth. It was an unusual thing in those days to let the children be first.

Although we did not live physically close to each other after my freshman year at college, Mother corresponded with me through long, detailed letters. At least once a week we wrote back and forth and we discussed the happenings of our lives and we shared ideas and thoughts with each other. Her letters always helped me stay connected in my mind with my North Carolina family and they helped me to persevere in difficult times.

Mother appreciated the little things in life like a handmade valentine collage. I sent her the one I had made as a demonstration for the children in my class one year. She loved hearing stories of what the children in my class said or did. The last time she visited a class of mine she must have been in her late seventies or early eighties. It was an exciting day as she taught the children to make folded airplanes and fly them!

Mother knew that methods in teaching change and she never insisted that how she learned to teach was the right or best way although she had found it to be a successful way. She would even laugh as she told the story about a "very old" first-grade teacher who had been many years at the school where she was first hired to teach. As a new teacher, Mother had learned the latest methods, and she was shocked to find this teacher was still using an outdated way to teach reading! Yet, low and behold, at the end of the year all those children could read just as well as hers!

So if Mother were alive and read this book, she would agree and disagree, she would have ideas to add and questions to ask. And when it was all said and done, she would smile and be grateful to have had her own contributions to make to the lives of so many little children. And she would be happy for me that I likewise have known that joy.

FIRST PREPARATION FOR TEACHING — LIFE AT THE DOUGHTON HOUSE

Of course, my unofficial preparation for working with young children had come from living with my parents who were very focused on all little children. Neighborhood children seemed to sense that my parents liked and respected them and they in turn seemed to like my parents. Maybe we will discover there is a gene that helps us relate well to little children. Possibly I inherited that! I always enjoyed little children and a lot of things that most little children like such as stories, dramatic play, arts and crafts, and games. As I grew up, I enjoyed telling and reading stories to my youngest sister, Jo Wayne, and I liked babysitting the neighbors' children and entertaining them.

Several years ago while visiting my sister Martha in North Carolina, she took me to visit an art museum in Raleigh. After looking at the paintings, we were surprised and delighted to see a neighbor from our childhood days in Durham. In conversation, the neighbor mentioned that she often thought of our family as the "Wild Doughtons." What? I had never considered us wild. We knew the manners of the time and practiced them if company arrived. But wild—I guess we must have appeared so. In retrospect, there were unusual camping rigs parked from time to time in front of our house. Dad had made them for our summer trips to explore other states. Once we even went to Canada. Our yard was a little "wild." It was not neatly trimmed as were the neighbors' yards.

Recently I called my sister Martha to discuss this "wild" description of us. When she answered the phone she was down on the floor playing with her youngest grandchild, Austin. I could hear him making noises in the background. They both seemed to be having such a grand time playing with Austin's toys. Yes, Martha has it too—that Doughton delight and connection to little children. I asked Martha about what she thought about the "wild" as descriptive of our family. I told her what I had mentioned in this paper about the yard and the camping machines. She said as she remembered it, our yard was mostly rocks and sticks and only a little grass— even worse than I remembered. She added that maybe "wild" had also to do with the fact that children seemed to feel free to play at our house and our parents allowed for spontaneity. She said she had friends who had told her that they always had liked coming to play at her house because it was a fun. Martha added that she thought Mother and Daddy never appeared to be controlling or interfering in our play, but in retrospect they were managing the situation in some unobtrusive fashion, not noticeable so much to us at the time. I have often had similar thoughts about their methods; there was a method in the non-method.

I did not decide early on working with young children as my career. I remember thinking when I was about eleven that I would like to be a first-grade teacher like Mother had been. Then in high school I loved math a lot, but could not really think of a career with it that I would enjoy. I liked most subjects except English.

My Education To Become A Teacher

COLLEGE –
DUKE UNIVERSITY AND
THE UNIVERSITY OF TENNESSEE

When I began my college work at Duke, I chose a double major in history and religion. My freshman classes were interesting, but by the middle of that year, I could not see how history and all the rest that goes with liberal arts would be very practical in "helping others," which now was a major interest of mine. I had always loved art and traveling too. How in the world could I have it all? I felt a little like the man in *Millions of Cats* by Wanda Gag, who wanted to choose all the cats.

Finally I decided to change my major to home economics because that would be a practical field that I could work in to "help others," and if I got married and had lots of children like I hoped, then whatever I learned could be put to use there. Also if I got to be a missionary, which was another hope, I thought a home economics background would be helpful. Anyway, that was my thinking and I proceeded to apply to the University of Tennessee because as a liberal arts school, Duke had no home economics classes. As an added bonus the Home Economics School at UT had a craft department; by taking six classes in crafts I could get a specialization area in it. So I could have my art interest to pursue also.

Things went pretty well at UT; most of the home economics subjects were not as hard for me as the liberal arts courses had been. Probably this was true because I had had a lot of hands-on experience in sewing, and some in cooking. Also, most of the home economics courses did not require lots of reading and writing, which were not my strong suits. We had many science courses which I found interesting, and they were not too difficult for me due to my strong math background. But now I missed the rigors of academic challenge. Now I began to think maybe I should study philosophy. Also, I was recognizing that there was some "looking down your nose" at the home economics girls in other areas on campus—maybe we weren't so smart—was that why we chose home economics? I did not like the feeling of being looked down upon.

So I asked for a conference with Dean Harris and I was given an appointed time to see her. "Well, Sudie, what's bothering you?" she queried. I didn't mention the part about the "low status" I felt the home economics girls had in other areas of the university. Instead I just said something to the effect that I had decided I really needed to study philosophy. At that she looked at me with that stern smile of hers and said, "Let me tell you a story." She told me how she had majored in Latin and gone out to teach high school girls when she was a young woman. She said she realized most of the girls she was teaching needed to learn nutrition, cooking, sewing, home management, child development, etc. far more than they needed Latin. So she went back to college to study something in the field of home economics.

She then looked at me and said something to the effect, "You need to finish your home economics education. You will have something specific accomplished and you will be able to find work. You can study philosophy all your life. It will take a lifetime to know much about that anyway."

Wow, what power and presence she had! I bet nobody looked down on her. I followed her advice and have been grateful that somebody stopped me in my tracks and helped me focus on finishing a course I had chosen. So I continued to study all the subjects which would prepare me to be a home economics teacher. Interesting that in most of these classes there was specific teaching about specific things. However, in the Child Development classes the teaching seemed to have come from a different model. I found those classes particularly interesting.

In the first Child Development class we went to lectures, studied theories, and observed the children in the lab school. I remember sitting on a little stool behind a one-way screen in the observation booth which was at one end of the big room. From the booth you could not see or hear everything. I peered and strained sometimes to no avail. I wished I could be in the middle of it all, not sitting and just watching. The demeanor of the head teachers and students working in the lab was more reserved and less interactive with the children than the adults I had known in my childhood. The college students working in the lab had to wear starched and pressed green smocks.

My Education To Become A Teacher

As a student, I had to choose one child to observe for my progress report. It was to include all the different areas of development: physical, social, emotional, etc. It was a little like all those observations my mother had written up in my baby book. I'm not sure if this progress report was for the first or second class.

In my second Child Development class we actually got to work with the children. Now I wore the green smock. I remember distinctly one episode from that time. We had been advised not to use bribery or tricks to try to get the children to do things. After many days of sitting at lunch with a little girl who refused to drink her milk with all the pleasant suggestions I could think to make, I looked around and saw nobody watching, so I said to the little girl in a quiet voice, "I bet you can't drink that milk before I count to ten." She downed it in no time. I did and still do not believe that bribes and tricks are a good idea as a rule, but I can't help smiling when I remember the giggle of that little girl as she finished that milk before I got to ten!

From classes and observations I was surprised to learn that the professors in Child Development at that time did not believe it necessary to teach and practice manners with children in an explicit way as had been done in my upbringing. Now the idea seemed to be that the children would pick it up from being around others who used good manners. And similar to the idea about manners, children were expected to pick up knowledge from an enriched environment with lots of books, puzzles, and other activities. Adults were not to take roles in the play of the children. They were to observe and redirect when necessary.

Things that could be observed easily, like physical skills, getting along or not with others, and doing things independently, were much studied at that time. There seemed to be a belief that teaching specific things such as numbers, letters, how to stand in line, etc. should wait for regular school. There was an emphasis on choice of play, on creative activities, and also on reducing frustration as much as possible. The best books for little children were considered those that were about the lives the children were presently living. These were called "Here and Now" books. Please, no scary characters like a Big Bad Wolf! The program seemed predicated on the idea that by having a satisfactory experience now, the children would naturally be ready for the next thing in their future, public school! It seemed like a reasonable assumption.

Of course as a part of my studies to become a home economics teacher I had several courses in general education as well as courses in how to teach home economics in high school, but I did not have methods courses in teaching specific curricula to preschool and kindergarten age children.

Comments and Thoughts

Although my initial feeling was dislike for observation, what I learned in the way of observation in those two Child Development courses has been of far reaching value. I have used those skills in all the places I have worked. In retrospect, maybe the ability to do a "scientific observation" was what the professors were most trying to teach. The need for that skill would never change although methods of working with young children might. As an elective, I took a third Child Development course. It was about science for young children.

The fact that I look with a critical eye today on some aspects of the university nursery schools in the late 1950s does not mean that the programs were ineffective for most of the children they served at that time. The emphases on choice of activities, many creative activities, enhancing social and physical skills, playing with minimal interference from adults, etc. were all a good balance with what the children received at home. At home they generally had: outspoken adults, traditional stories, learning little chores, learning manners, playing with neighborhood children in rather unstructured activities. The nursery school was in many ways a contrast to what the children experienced at home. But of course at home and at nursery school, adults believed in the abilities of the children and there was a basic structure, routine, and known expectations in both settings. Also the children at the lab schools generally came from families that valued education and were willing to pay for preschool and make the necessary transportation arrangements. Some recent research has shown that where parents have some responsibility, financially or otherwise, for the program their children attend, the children make better progress.

I was graduated from college in August 1959. I was thrilled that my first job would be with young children rather than high school students. I had lots of experience with little children, and

My Education To Become A Teacher

I had always enjoyed them. However, I only had a small amount of specific training for being a teacher of young children. I would have much to learn.

Part IV
First Job
Sweet Memorial Day Care in Chile
As a three-year missionary with the Methodist Church

For my two dear friends in Chile,
Sra. Haydee Escobar and Srta. Marta Martinez

Sra. Haydee was the "Professora" in the "Kindergarten," the room for three-to-six-year-olds at Sweet. Besides being a wonderful teacher, she is an accomplished musician, a loving mother and grandmother, and a faithful friend. She has corresponded with me since I left Chile in 1963.

Srta. Marta was the nurse at Sweet. She had grown up in Concepcion, Chile, where her father was the Methodist pastor. At Sweet, she took an interest in each child each day, and all the children trusted and loved her. She had a calmness in the middle of any accident or problem that helped the child to be less frightened and upset. Although the day care center at Sweet no longer exists, Srta. Marta still works with children and families in

Santiago. I love to receive her letters in which she shares with me some of her present experiences.

Foreword

I have written extensively about this experience because it has influenced every aspect of my life. Students at workshops have frequently asked me about the children in Chile, why I liked it so much there, what was the difference with our way of life, etc. Usually I have not had the time to give a good account. This is an effort to do so.

It is interesting to contemplate the hours that I was at Sweet and the actual time spent with the children and staff. We were together eleven months of the year, eight to ten hours a day. I lived at Sweet as well as working there. So I was with children more hours of the day and more months of the year than I have ever been in a job since. I ate three meals a day with other staff members and we often saw each other outside work hours. My friendship with Sra. Haydee and Srta. Marta was based on many hours of shared experiences and time.

Earlier in this book, I discussed a little about my work in Chile in the dedication to Margaret (Peggy) Becker for Part I and also in the write up on "Maria, the Silent, Expressionless Child." In some of the papers in Part II, I also mentioned some of my experiences in Chile.

It is important to clarify that Sweet Memorial had two separate parts: the day care center as one part and another section that was for young people preparing to be Christian workers. Those students also attended high school at night if they needed to. On that side of Sweet, the staff had club activities and group work for the neighborhood children as well as the classes for the young people going into Christian work. The building of the Second Methodist Church and the parsonage sat in between the two parts of Sweet.

FIRST IMPRESSIONS OF CHILE AND SWEET

It was late in the afternoon when my ship docked in the Chilean port of Valparaiso. The air seemed crisp and cool. It was

First Job - Sweet Memorial Day Cay In Chile

fall, sometime late April or early May. Walt Mason and Florence Prouty, Methodist missionaries in Santiago, greeted me as I got off the Grace Line freighter that had brought me to Chile.

We loaded my bags in the back of Walt's pick-up and headed for Santiago, a trip of about three hours. It was a paved highway. Valparaiso had been full of lights. So far this did not appear so different from home. Walt didn't talk much. Maybe he couldn't get a word in edgewise...Florence and I talked a lot. Florence was the missionary in charge of the day care part of Sweet where I would be working.

Santiago seemed huge. We drove through one section and then another and then several miles down a busy thoroughfare filled with buses, taxies, a few horse-drawn wagons, and finally we turned onto a cobblestone street. Halfway down the block we pulled up in front of a big grey stone building with a tall fence in front of it. There was a lock on the gate, a small walkway, a few steps, and two big doors, each with different locks. The floor in the entryway was a beautiful dark, red tile. A picture of Christ with the children was on the wall to the right.

Many people crowded around to greet me on the night of my arrival in April or May 1960. My room on the second floor was brightened by fresh flowers and fresh fruit and a container of water with a special glass. There was a kerosene stove to use in the evenings if I needed it.

Also on the second floor of this building was the dining room for the adults, the room for the babies, the apartment for Miss Prouty, Srta. Marta's room, and a guest room. On the third flood were dormitory rooms for many of the young women who worked at Sweet in the daytime and went to high school at night. Many of them had come up to Santiago from Methodist homes in rural areas of Chile. In another part of the third floor was the laundry, with its old style wringer-type washing machines, ironing boards, and a patio where the clothes could be hung to dry.

The main floor had a big hall and several offices: one for the secretary, one for the social worker, and one for Miss Prouty. Also there was an examining room for the doctor and a place for the dentist to work. There was a very small room for the seamstress. Off of the main hall to the left was the kitchen. Farther down the hall, then down a few steps, and the toddler room was on the right and the big room for the "three through sixes" on the left.

Next morning I was introduced to the one hundred children, some of the parents, and to the staff who didn't live at Sweet. The parents and children began arriving at seven o'clock. Babies were taken upstairs to their department, the only section that was heated in the winter. They were bathed after arrival and put in clothes provided by Sweet. The toddlers in their section were washed up and changed into little pink uniforms that had skirts. Both the boys and the girls in the toddler section wore these. I think primarily it was because it made using the potty much easier. (Little boys in Chile I saw on the streets were dressed in pants.) In the wintertime the children wore the uniform over their clothes to help stay warm. The uniforms for the older children were all dark blue, and the girls had dresses but the boys had little coverall-type uniforms with pants. It took a while for me to get used to all the uniforms! Children in all the schools in Chile wore uniforms.

One of the first things I noticed was how much the parents seemed to care about their children. They never seemed rushed. They were constantly talking to the children and usually smiling at them. Upon arrival each morning at Sweet, the parent and child greeted the staff with a friendly, yet formal good morning, *"Buenos dias,"* plus the name of the person. I was amazed as each mother looked expectantly at their baby or toddler and said, e.g., "Juanito, say *buenos dias a* Srta. Marta." And in this instance, Srta. Marta would greet the child with an affectionate, *"Buenos dias,* Juanito." Of course by the time the children could talk a little they were saying *"Buenos dias"* in response to an adult's greeting without any coaching whatsoever. I found this a charming and wonderful way to start each day. In retrospect I believe that it had good vibes for all concerned and it was an important ritual in treating each person individually with a culturally understood and approved greeting. It set the tone for the day.

THE STAFF OF THE DAY CARE CENTER

Florence Prouty, the *directora*, was a nurse by original education and training. Now she had mainly administrative duties. Everyday

First Job - Sweet Memorial Day Cay In Chile

Miss Prouty would make rounds to all the different departments to check each place out and look for anything that needed to be corrected. And in the rest of her time, she was working with visitors, studying the finances, and figuring out ways to raise money, etc. Letters had to be written to churches in the United States that contributed to our mission. Relationships with "the committee," an elite group of women in Santiago who raised funds to help with the day care center, had to be maintained, a pilot medical and dental program at the barrio San Ramon had to be managed. She must have been a genius in organization and in training people to work. Since I was not very trainable and did not follow specific directions well, sometimes I felt like "a barnacle on the hind-end of progress." I think she finally figured out what I could do and assigned me to those jobs.

Srta. Marta did most of the daily work of being sure that everything was working smoothly and well in the infant and toddler sections which had three assistance in each section. She also worked with the doctor and dentist who came to Sweet occasionally to see the children. There was a social worker who came from time to time also. Srta. Marta was the link between her and our children's families.

Srta. Thelma was our secretary. She alwasy seemed cheerful and lovely. She took care of all the records, phone calls, and general office work.

Sra. Haydee was the "Professora" of the kindergarten. In this book I will not use the term "kindergarten" for that room since in the States we use that word exclusively for the year before first grade and it might prove confusing to the readers about the ages of the children in that room. Those children were three, four, five, and six years old. There were three young women who usually assisted Sra. Haydee with the fifty children in that department. During my second and third year in Chile, I worked in that room also most of the time.

Sra. Rosario headed up the kitchen staff. She was a wonderful cook. She had an assistant to help her. She and Miss Prouty had both been at Sweet for many years, maybe longer than anyone else. Most of the professional staff and the young women working at Sweet had three meals a day there, and the one hundred children were fed three times also. I'm not sure who invented the meal plans, maybe Florence. Those meals were nutritionally excellent according to all the standards we are aware of today, good tasting, and economical. We had fruit for dessert at the midday meal. Sugary items were not a daily fare. They were only for special events. I liked Sra. Rosario from the start, she seemed to like me, and I noticed she kept an eye out for me in a nurturing way.

Sra. Merecedes, our seamstress, made the uniforms for the children and the large white aprons for the young women at Sweet who were not professional staff. Those starched and pressed aprons were reminiscent of those green smocks we had at the UT lab. (Remember, the smocks were only worn by us students, not the teachers or professors.)

And there was Martita, a young woman who did not live at Sweet but who arrived early each morning for her day's work. She cleaned all the rooms on the second floor, mine included, and she did special errands for Miss Prouty. I noticed she too smiled and greeted the children by name if she passed them in the halls. I grew to like Martita a lot and I was appreciative of the care she gave my room and me.

Our janitor, Carlos, was the only grown man around—unless some missionary stopped by to visit as they did quite often. Carlos arrived early each day and brought the fresh bread for everyone's breakfast. He had picked up the bread at the corner bakery. And I remember that bread well; it was crusty and hard and hot from the oven. Yum, yum!

LIFE IN THE BIG ROOM

After all the hugs and greetings, the children changed into their uniforms or put them on over their clothes if it was cold. The adults in this room helped with the clothes. After the greetings and clothes-changing, each child could choose an activity. These activities reminded me of the ones at the UT lab nursery school. There was a big area with three cases of unit blocks. There was a house area with a small stove, baby dolls and little beds, an ironing board and iron, little tables and chairs, etc. In another area there were shelves with puzzles and another shelf with books. There was an easel for painting on large blank newsprint. There were crayons and paper. And similar to the situation in the lab school, the adults observed and helped the children when necessary, but in general they refrained from participating in the play. However, everything seemed more "lively" than the nursery school lab had been. Of course, there were more children in the room, a wider age range, and the children belonged to a culture that was very oral and spontaneous.

Peggy Becker, mentioned earlier, was the individual who had initiated using this style of preschool program at Sweet. I do not think that this type of program was in place elsewhere in Chile in the early '60s. Peggy had volunteered to work at Sweet soon after she and her husband had first come to Chile in the late 1950s. She had given hours of work plus she had contributed many of the items to be used. She had the unit blocks and other things like the furniture for the house corner made to specification by a local wood craftsman in Chile. She had brought many classic children's books from the States such as *Blueberries for Sal, Trees are Nice, Make Way for Ducklings,* etc. We translated these as best we could. Peggy had taught Sra. Haydee how to work with this type of program and then they together taught the "assistants" and later the children how to use this "choice type program."

Sra. Haydee Escobar had been at Sweet probably fifteen years at least. When she entered the room at nine a.m. each day, I could just feel the children relax as they greeted her and felt her presence in the room. She had that same **quality of calmness combined with dignity and purpose and warmth that I have noticed many excellent teachers possess.** Sra. Haydee told me she had been taught to use many different programs for young children over the years. I think she had adapted to them all. And I am sure she had found ways to add her own spark to each method.

Soon after nine, we officially began the day in the big room with opening exercises. The tables and house area equipment were pushed to the side and the children made an enormous circle. We began with singing the Chilean National Anthem with Sra. Haydee's rousing piano accompaniment. With what enthusiasm we all sang! It was a momentous beginning for even the most usual day. As a part of the opening program, we said prayers and sang children's hymns and sometimes we sang Chilean folk songs or had musical games. With the sun streaming in through the big bank of windows, shining on the fifty children gathered in a huge circle in the big room, I felt a connectedness to the whole world.

Once we had a large group of Methodist pastors from the States visiting Sweet and they were in the room about the time of the morning exercises. As the children finished singing "Jesus Me Ama," all those grown and dignified men spontaneously responded, singing "Jesus Loves Me" in English, blending their strong tenor and bass voices as one great echo to the children's hymn. Wow! It was awesome.

Back to the routine...after the opening exercises, the children were divided into two groups according to age. One group went outside to play for about an hour while the other group played inside with the activities. Before their inside activity time was over, the older children had a story at a group time led by Sra. Haydee. On Mondays, she gave a Sunday school lesson to the children, often telling a Bible story with the illustrations from large pictures or by using flannel board characters. After story time, the older children then went out to play and the younger ones then came inside to build with blocks, do puzzles, play in the house corner, etc. At the end of their activity time, the younger children gathered for a story time. I frequently read to that group.

I often tried to put my observation skills to use since that was one thing I knew how to do. One of my earliest observations was watching a little three-year-old girl draw pictures each day as her very first activity usually about seven-thirty a.m. In the beginning, her pictures were scribble designs, or so they appeared to me. After several months of drawing each morning, I began to notice that a big rectangular shape was beginning to appear in all of her pictures. From week to week I could see her pictures develop. She would color in various parts of the shape. After a few more weeks, doors appeared and I could tell it was a house. Over an extended period of time she kept adding more details to the house pictures. (One of her houses is on the front cover. It is the house near the center of the collage.) In all my forty years, I never observed another three-year-old choosing the same work or activity so consistently as the first thing to do each day and continuing with it such a long time. This child also participated in all of the other activities as the day went on. She seemed very vibrant as were most

First Job - Sweet Memorial Day Cay In Chile

of the children at Sweet in spite of the fact that they were from homes with limited financial resources.

The unit block building by the children at Sweet was the most complicated I have ever seen anywhere. They made huge structures. One day the children made a circus with three large circular enclosures. They went over to the house center and invited the children there to come to the circus. They pretended to be lions and bears doing their acts, etc. Another time they used the cylinder-shaped blocks (on the rounded part) as a foundation for a building which they could later roll from one place to another by removing cylinders from the back of the building as it rolled off and placing those in front so there would always be cylinders under it!

Lunch was served at about noon. Afterwards, the tables and chairs were pushed aside and the cots were brought out for nap time, which lasted from about one until three p.m. At nap time only one of the assistants stayed in the room with the fifty children and since the children were usually sleeping, the person on nap duty had an ironing board set up and ironed uniforms! No wasted time here.

The professional staff and personnel not on nap duty had two hours off after lunch. Many of them probably spent that time preparing for their night classes at a nearby high school. Sra. Haydee, Srta. Marta, Srta. Thelma, the secretary, and I continued to sit at the table and drink coffee or tea after the completion of our midday main meal. Miss Prouty stayed for some of the conversation now and then. I enjoyed an extra hour just to talk and listen about current events and other topics of interest. Listening to conversation among the same people everyday helped me greatly in learning Spanish. I was able to understand and participate more and more as the months went by. In retrospect this special time every day of relaxed conversation among friends was something I missed greatly when I came home. Now I am fortunate if I experience it even once a week!

After the extended lunch time and free time, we returned to duties. In the big room with the fifty children, the assistants (called the personnel) were helping the children get up and were putting away the cots and getting the room back in order. Often, some of the children played outside after lunch and nap time. Outside there was a huge jungle gym for climbing, big wooden boxes that the children could build with, a swing and a bar, see-saws, a sand box, a water table, and a walking and jumping board. Sra. Haydee sometimes used the afternoon time to teach the children more musical games, folklore songs, dances, and little plays and poems, especially if a holiday program was "in the works."

HOLIDAY PROGRAMS

The children always put on a polished and well-done program for the parents and for our special committee, the group of North American and Chilean women who helped raise money for the day care center. Each year the programs varied. Sra. Haydee's ingenious ideas and choreography and musical talents seem to have no end. Many children learned all the parts as they participated in practicing for the programs.

In my mind of the early 1960s I puzzled over what I saw and experienced. What I had understood from my limited study of Child Development in the late 1950s was that these sorts of productions were not good for young children. I discussed this with Peggy Becker and she agreed with me that in this setting she saw no ill effects from these programs. What we did see were the good effects of the children's learning how to memorize, how to project their voices, learning what "this" holiday was all about, paying attention to detail, learning to sing songs and how to do the folk dances of their country, how to practice as a group and wait their turns, etc.

I think the fact that the children were in Sweet for many years, approximately eight to ten hours a day for eleven months of the year promoted their sense of security and confidence. Also from the moment they entered Sra. Haydee's class they were receiving musical education. The threes and fours had participated in a general way in all those songs and games and dances during the morning exercises before they learned and performed the more complicated and solo parts for the programs when they were five and six. **In other words the children were ready to learn what they were being taught. A foundation had been laid. Interesting practice sessions that proceeded in a sequenced and non-**

threatening fashion helped complete the preparation for each holiday program.

SWEET AS A MODEL DAY CARE AND
MY RELATIONSHIPS WITH CHILEAN TEACHERS

Our day care center had been chosen by the universities in Santiago as a place to visit and observe. Students studying to be doctors and nurses and social workers came on a regular basis. Students studying to be preschool teachers from the University of Chile came to observe. Several teachers did their practice teaching with us. There was an organization of preschool teachers in Santiago. I attended their meetings and programs from time to time. From my association with other teachers and people in preschool education, such as Alicia Navarro and one of the university students, Isolde Brand, I learned a few things about preschool education in general in Chile.

I noticed the Chilean college students and teachers in preschool education knew a lot about European methods of teaching. They seemed surprised that I did not know much about Froebel and Montessori, etc. Of course, I had only had three Child Development courses and several general education courses, but interestingly enough when I came home and did my master's I still did not hear much about the European educators of "yesteryear" or the current ones, for that matter.

I remember one of the things that the university students studying to be preschool teachers did was to make illustrations on large sheets of cardboard. These would be used to show the children as they told the traditional folk tales such as *The Three Bears, Little Red Riding Hood,* etc. The fact that the students made these reminded me of things my mother had made for teaching her first graders. Also, I found it interesting that the focus of the literature for children the university students were using at that time was the traditional folk tales. They certainly provided a common link to the experiences of older children and adults who had learned these stories in childhood. And they were full of interesting characters and predicaments that children relate to. Some recent educators have pointed out that in the States we need to tell our children traditional stories that everyone has heard as well as reading the newer children's books.

In the 1960s, there were some books published in Chile that included songs and games for little children. Sra. Haydee used some of these. I looked around in the bookstores in Santiago for story books for young children written in Spanish. I did find a few. One was the story of life on a farm in Spain. It had lovely colorful illustrations. It went though the whole year explaining seasonal changes, special work involved, etc. Another one was about life in the big city and it was folded in such a way that it opened up and opened up again and again, adding new views of the city with each unfolding. These books were shades of the "Here and Now" books, but they seemed more creatively put together than books in that category I had known in the States.

SOME THOUGHTS ABOUT FOOD FOR CHILDREN

At Sweet, the children were given milk for breakfast and possibly hot cereal. My memory is not clear on that. Most of the children had been given bread by their parents before they arrived at Sweet. The noon meal for the children was a hardy soup with vegetables and meat and sometimes beans and rice all ground up together. The evening meal was another soup. Some of the children probably ate again with their parents later in the evening. The children ate with relish. They were not picky like so many of the children I had observed in the States. Most of the children at our day care appeared healthy and they had good attendance.

Had the high sugar and greatly refined food frequently fed children in this country diminished their desire for good, nutritious food? Could the picky eating of children I had known in the States have something to do with lack of fresh air and exercise? Could it be that grinding all that food up and serving more or less the same consistency every day was to the children's liking? Could it be that living and playing in non-heated rooms had something to do with it? In the wintertime that hot soup would have been particularly satisfying, I believe. Also, that soup was something that would stay warm easily as the bowls were one by one ladled up and put in front of the children awaiting them. And it was easy to eat, no changing back and forth to forks and knives. And most of all, with every bite the children were receiving good nourishment. There is much to consider here. In retrospect I remember a certain great "gusto" to life that was a Chilean characteristic. Maybe that also had contributed to the children's enjoyment of good food.

AFFECTS OF DAY CARE

I was amazed at how well the children at Sweet did in spite of, or possibly because of, day care. I had been taught in the late '50s in university in the States that day care was not usually a good option for most young children. The reason given was that infants and toddlers need the care and attention of a consistent loving and nurturing figure such as mother. At Sweet the staff was consistently caring and nurturing. At Sweet there was not much turn-over in staff, so the children saw the same adults each day and throughout their years at Sweet. The relatively slower pace and cultural belief that children were very important meant that when most parents were with the children they seemed to pay them a lot of attention, etc. So there were major cultural differences that probably helped these children adjust and do fine in day care.

As I have emphasized, all the people working at Sweet seemed to take a very positive and loving interest in each child. Interestingly enough, at the same time each of the "personnel" had a few children that warranted an extra word or longer hug. The children too seemed to have their favorites among the adults. It surprised me that I did not see bad results from this. Maybe because it was held in check and not noticeable unless you observed everyday and often the child receiving the extra attention was a particularly needy child. In a society where most children are highly valued and loved, maybe the children are not threatened by this kind of thing or so competitive for the time and attention of adults.

Even though the girls who worked at Sweet made low salaries and had busy lives, going to night school, etc., they appeared to enjoy life and usually seemed to be contented with themselves and their work. After all, children were important! And they did not have their own children yet to be preoccupied with. I think also that the overall attitudes and underlying sense of acceptance and enjoyment of life of the Chilean people influenced the growth and development of the children in a positive way.

I noticed that on the buses in Chile if a mother got irritated with her child, another woman would frequently offer to help by talking with the child or holding a baby, etc. Families frequently called their children by endearing terms, *"Preciosa," "Muy linda,"* etc. I observed families walking in the parks and the mothers and fathers beaming with pride and interest in their children. Many children in Chile had consistent, loving, and caring relationships with people other than their parents; e.g., nursemaids, grandmothers, aunts, and friends. I once visited in a home far from Santiago where there was a six- or seven-year-old niece whose parents lived in Santiago and she was living with her aunt and family for an indefinite period of time just because she liked it there and everyone was delighted to have her.

OTHER THOUGHTS AND MEMORIES

In Chile in my time there, children were not necessarily privy to the adult world. The children did have a known and accepted place in the life of the family and community. They were often fed separately and put to bed before the adults ate, but that in no way diminished their importance. Most children in Chile seemed to accept adult authority readily and only on very, very rare occasions did I hear a child argue with an adult. Spanish has two forms of "you," the formal, *ud.*, and the informal, *tu*. Children learned early when to use which form, and they never used *tu* for an adult. Maybe that helped remind them who was in charge.

When my three years in Chile were over, I was feasted and partied and given gifts and mementos and in my mind now I had the even larger gifts of a new language, loving another country, many new friends, and the "hands-on education" of three years working under the tutelage of two great teachers, Sra. Haydee and Peggy Becker. It was indeed a life-enhancing experience. Of course there were many other wonderful experiences in Chile other than my work at Sweet. These included working with young people at a church, traveling up and down the country on the trains and buses to visit other towns and missions, seeing movies from around the world when they came to Santiago, and having lunch at the YWCA on Mondays which was my afternoon "off" from regular duties at Sweet. In May 1963 I headed home on a Norwegian freighter, the Thor Odland.

SPECIFIC PREPARATION TO SERVE AS AN "L.A. 3"

The Methodist Church (specifically the Women's Society of Christian Service) gave me good education for my work in Chile. For readers who are interested in the specific preparation I received, I have included the following information.

I had not been able to attend the group training for L.A.3's (short-term missionaries assigned to Latin America) because it was held in the summer before my graduation from college. I was sorry that I had missed getting to know other young people who would be "short-termers" like me, but in some ways I was glad I had such extensive class work such as a full quarter at Scarritt College with many regular missionaries and graduate foreign students in the field of Christian work.

The classes at Scarritt included linguistics, social anthropology, history of missions, social group work with practicum at Bethlehem Center, and maybe one other class. Both the linguistics course and social anthropology opened up new worlds of thought for me. Linguistics taught us how to learn a foreign language by listening, very much the way children learn their mother tongue. I was an oral learner and I had never done well in the old way of reading and memorizing foreign language. In this class, we were not studying the language where we were going…we were learning about languages and how they are put together. I spent lab hours listening to Japanese tapes and trying to pick up repetitive sounds, etc. It was an activity I recognized my brain connected to and liked.

The social anthropology class focused on the theories of Radcliffe-Brown and we had to write an extensive paper about one tribe of people, discussing their way of life in the context of the Radcliffe-Brown theories of culture. We could not study any group of people in the specific part of the world where we were going. This was to be a part of our broader understanding of how societies work, not a follow the guide 1, 2, 3 of what to think about a specific situation. My paper was on the Bemba tribe in Africa.

In retrospect, most of my education from home and school had been about getting a big picture and understanding the broad contexts of everything. There had been some exceptions namely in the memorization of arithmetic tables and later in some of my home economics classes which had been very specific. I wonder about these different kinds of knowledge and different methods of learning. It seems to me, in the "big picture" type of education, it is up to the student to pick out from what the teacher says, and to pick out of the texts and to sift out of the class discussion, what is important. I had learned how to do that and I often found it distasteful to be told explicitly what to do.

After Scarritt I still had more education…three months of intensive, specific Spanish language training. I was sent to an interdenominational language school in San Jose, Costa Rica. I did not do so well in that school as most of the classes were still following methods of teaching that focused on reading and writing and grammar. However, I enjoyed the beautiful countryside, the colorful geometric floor tiles, the marimba music, houses painted many colors, bright birds, and strong coffee as well as the sweets served at break each morning at the language school.

The linguistic bug had bitten me and I knew I could learn Spanish "that way." Memorizing Bible verses in Spanish and getting the intonation right…that was the one class I excelled in at the institute. The language school also offered me a chance to meet missionaries of many different ideas and denominations. Following language school, I was off to Chile aboard a Grace Line freighter that I boarded in Panama.

Part V
Graduate School, University Teaching, Parent Co-op, Head Start

In memory of "Aunt Mattie," **Martha Rebecca Doughton**

One of us children could not say the "m" for Mattie and so she became "Tattie" to the kids in our family. She was our father's only sister, about eleven years his senior. I could not recount all the visits to Tattie's house and all the influences she had on my life. But I will mention a few. It did not matter when we arrived, unexpectedly or planned, things were always lovely. Everything was in its place. There was always something special that could be fixed that would be good to eat. She served the food on china plates and she always used her sterling silver. There was a bottom drawer in one of the cabinets with the toys for the children to play with. These were the old toys left over from my dad's childhood! There was Great-grandmother's stereoscope and the pictures from all over the world. There were beautiful hand-woven coverlets or handmade quilts on the beds. It was a house with wonderful textures, fine fragrances, and visual delights. Tattie was also an avid recycler. She saved paper bags and twine from packages and they were all neatly stashed away in a closet in the kitchen.

When I was a teenager and Tattie was at an age that most people would have been retired, she had an active business as an interior decorator. In one of her antique wardrobes she kept all the fabric samples, and what fun they were to see and feel!

Tattie had been an English teacher for most of her career. I heard that she was the first woman to get a master's degree in English from the University of North Carolina. Her living room held two large bookcases filled with Shakespeare's works, books by other famous authors, history books, family photograph albums, etc. As a child I loved the photograph albums of all the great-aunts and uncles, grandparents, and others. From looking at all the pictures, I surmised there had been a lot of people and a lot of life before I was born.

I remember a happening from the 1950s when someone had asked Tattie to come and "substitute-teach" in a high school English class. She had not taught in many years, but she went anyway. She told me it was a rowdy class and she was having trouble gaining control until she informed the students that they had better pay attention and listen and not get her upset because she might have a "fit" and a "bad one" at that! She said the kids calmed down. Years later she saw one of the boys from the class and he asked her if she really had fits.

My last great story about Tattie happened when Mother was in the Moravian Home in Winston. I was visiting Mother and we happened to be riding in the elevator one day. Mother introduced us to the other person in the elevator. The woman introduced herself, and then she asked, "Are you kin to Mattie Doughton?" I explained that she was my aunt. Suddenly a big smile broke across her face and with a twinkle in her eye and a faraway look, she added, "Oh, my, we were all such young girls at Salem College... Miss Doughton taught us Shakespeare and took us to worlds undreamed and unknown."

Foreword

I have grouped graduate school and my years in university teaching, co-ops, and Head Start together because in all of these situations the same basic philosophy about young children and the same methods for teaching were being used. Briefly, it was that each child was unique and special; we needed to observe each child carefully; we should use calm and thoughtful ways to interact with children while consistently encouraging their growth and development in all areas. The best preschool environment for young children would have many interesting activities and many choices for the child. Music and story times that were teacher led would be kept fairly short in keeping with the child's limited attention span. Naturally there were some changes and modifications of the basic design for a good preschool program during the twenty years that I taught under this umbrella. I tried to mention some of them as I became aware of them in various work experiences.

GRADUATE SCHOOL

During my study to get my master's degree in child development, I worked as a graduate assistant grading papers for professors as well as going to classes. My "not-so-hot" reading and writing skills meant much of the work took me a long time to accomplish. My math skills honed in solid geometry and trig back in high school stood me in good stead and carried me through statistics and critiquing the statistics used in research. It was a good thing I had a strong suit. The fact that I had been working with preschool-age children for three years before I came to graduate school seemed also to be a great advantage. Most of the other students in the program had arrived straight from finishing college.

There had been some changes in the lab school since my undergraduate classes. For one thing, the green smocks had disappeared. There were different teachers in the three-year-old class and in the four-year-old class. A kindergarten lab had been added. I thought the teachers were more interactive with the children than what I remembered from the 1950s.

Dr. Highberger, the head of the Child Development Department, arranged for me to do a practicum as a graduate student in a kindergarten that was located in a church in a Knoxville suburb. Tennessee did not yet have public school kindergarten.

I remember one day all these little boys asked me if I would play with them and be the "Martian." I said yes, and they all attacked me! Now I knew a reason for that rule about not taking a role in the children's play! Wow, the children in that kindergarten all had lots of vitality and those little boys were strong! The teacher was Nancy Moore and, similar to Sra. Haydee and those other good teachers, she had **charm, dignity, and purpose** in her demeanor as well as warmth and friendliness. In that kindergarten there was an interesting program with creative art activities, many craft projects, songs, stories, blocks, house play area, etc. They did observe holidays and learn traditional songs and crafts for those times. It was not so different from the program at Sweet with the exception that these holiday celebrations did not include "polished" performances by the children.

I believe at the UT lab school we did not have any holiday celebrations or holiday crafts circa 1964. I wish I had thought to ask Dr. Highberger more about the "holiday" issue. The holidays had been a wonderful part of my childhood and certainly a great part of life for children in Chile. I was glad to revisit them at Nancy's kindergarten!

Many of my graduate classes were about research and how to "do" research. My research was about children's choices for illustrations in picture books—whether they liked stylized or realistic art work. When we looked at the data for all the children taken at each of the various "choice presentations" there was no decided preference for the realistic or stylized picture.

One of the interesting things we discovered was that boys tended to change their preferences and the girls tended to choose the same type of picture each time they were given the choice. A friend of mine in graduate studies in nutrition told me of some research that had found those same differences in boys and girls when they were offered a plate with various food items and reoffered it several weeks later. The girls tended to choose the same things; the boys tended to choose different foods. I have often wondered about those findings. Writing my thesis was difficult, but I learned a lot about the process of research and potential difficulties involved in it. The oral exam was fun and an easier venue for me, but I don't remember learning as much from it as I did from the written part that had caused me much work and struggle.

Graduate School, University Teaching, Parent Co-op, Head Start

LAB TEACHER AND INSTRUCTOR AT UT

The University of Tennessee hired me as an instructor. In the mornings I taught classes to undergraduates such as literature for children, children's art, and the class for students working in the kindergarten. In the afternoons I was the head teacher in our kindergarten lab. I was also in charge of making up menus and overseeing the ordering of food for our nursery school lunch program. We had an experienced cook and experienced assistant to help with many things at the lab school. We had a nurse to check the children each day when they arrived for class.

The afternoon kindergarten lab was held in one of the rooms used for the nursery school children in the mornings. The children came Monday through Friday and the program lasted three or four hours. We had a long activity time inside with many choices for the children: puzzles, books, house play area, unit block area, easel painting, crayons and paper, etc. There was no problem providing and cleaning up from many creative art activities like real clay or finger painting because of the help available from support staff and students. Outside we had a beautiful large playground with grass and trees. There was a little sidewalk meandering through the area. Children could ride tricycles and pull wagons. There were also many pieces of moveable equipment that could be set up in a variety of ways for climbing and dramatic play.

Students working in the lab would plan a group of activities around a certain theme. I remember interesting units on the solar system, birds, the way we get our mail, etc. When studying the solar system we made a basketball-size ball out of paper mache and painted it yellow with splashes of red, orange, and blue here and there. We made an earth about the size of a marble and the other planets to that same scale. We took these out on our playground. One person would hold the sun in the center of this big area. Some other child would walk with the earth around the far perimeter of that playground. It was exciting and awesome to think about these perspectives. We assumed the children were enjoying these activities and learning at the same time.

President Kennedy was killed during one of the years I taught at UT. Also one child had lost a parent in a terrible accident that year. My kindergarten children enacted "funerals" off and on all that winter. I suspected they had seen the TV coverage of Kennedy's funeral and heard adults and older children discussing it. Of course, for the child who had lost a parent, death was all very close and real. We buried a dead bird with much solemnity and sorrow. We sang and cried over every dead bug. I felt it was healing. For that reason, I did not discourage the children from their role playing of something serious and sad.

In the '60s and '70s I was very interested in children's creativity and in their ability to take initiative in all of their activities. These were also major emphases in the university preschool programs of which I was a part. Some children in that time lived fairly constricted and "proper" lives and did not have opportunities to do things "their way." Being adventuresome and trying new things was a challenge. I remember a child who was horrified at the idea of cracking the egg shell so he could put the egg in the cookie dough. After discussing it, demonstrating how to do it, telling him I would help if need be, he tried and he seemed pleased with his achievement!

In those years in the lab school at UT, we resisted teaching anything specific about numbers or letters to the preschool children. We thought that the numbers and letters would be better taught in first grade. We did use number concepts with the children and counted out things together like the three eggs for the cookies. We also used songs and finger plays that had numbers as a part of them. We tried to provide an enriched environment for the children with many things to interest them and to support their general development. In retrospect this had been true of the program my friend, Peggy Becker, had introduced at Sweet; we made no effort to teach numbers or letters in any specific way even to the five and six year olds.

At UT in the 1960s, if a child had social, emotional, or physical problems, we observed those, gathered data, and did a staffing of the child with Dr. Highberger and others who had a broad range of knowledge as well as having observed this child. We would share our observations and then invent a plan of action usually involving encouragement, redirection if necessary, and positive reinforcement. We did not use time-outs as such. We never openly called a child "down" or discussed misbehavior in front of the other children. The adult tried to stay near the child who had the problem so that the appropriate intervention could take place when needed.

This system was usually effective for many reasons. We had trained and experienced head teachers plus student helpers that gave us a ratio of about four or five children to one adult. We never had more than two children with serious problems in the same group. We had more children we were concerned about because they were **shy** or **not creative** than children who demonstrated aggressive behavior toward others.

I remember seeing a parent of a child who had been in our lab kindergarten the previous year. The child was now in first grade. I asked him how things were going. He seemed displeased. He said, "Your school did not teach my child how to stand in line and he got in trouble at school the first week." I wondered about that and also comments from other parents of our alums who said their children were marked down for not following instructions 100% in their coloring.

The example about the coloring as told to me by her mother was as follows. The child was told to color the ball red. She had done that but she had added a blue stripe. The teacher said it was wrong. Luckily, that child told her mother and her mother was able to help her understand the situation. The mother explained to her why she thought the teacher wanted the children to follow the instructions without adding anything else. Her mother also told her that she liked her art work a lot and that at home she could draw and color her "own way." This is an example of the importance of children having someone to listen to them and to help make sense out of what they are experiencing. Also the second parent did not overreact to the problem or seem threatened by its existence.

Our kindergarten lab program at UT did not have enough children. I think it was because there were many good private kindergartens in the various parts of town. Transportation back and forth to the center of town each afternoon was problematic for some families. I believed having more children in the class was important. I got permission to hunt for children in the immediate university neighborhood. I knocked on lots of doors, but I only found one family, a single father with four children, who showed any interest in sending a child to kindergarten. His youngest boy enrolled in our class. Bill, the father, would come early to pick up Lucky; he would sit in the observation booth to observe. I thought, of course, that he was a very dedicated father. My life took a decided turn in many ways as we married the following fall and in the summer of 1966 we went to live in Montana.

Over the years the children, Linda, Clifford, Lucky, and Janet all have helped to keep my feet on the ground so to speak. I could not stay entirely in an ivory tower of theory and thought, "ideal programs," and research about family life and children!

MY WORK AT THE UNIVERSITY OF MONTANA

Soon after our arrival in Montana, the Home Economics Department at the University of Montana hired me to teach some of their child development and family life courses. Generally I worked half-time so that I could be home when the children got out of school. Every quarter I taught a course that was an overview of the life cycle using Eric Erickson's eight stages of life. I frequently taught a senior seminar in issues in family relations. Over the years I experimented with different texts and supplementary materials for all my classes. In the overview of life course, I required the students to observe in our preschool and kindergarten labs.

At times I conducted workshops and short courses on art activities or literature for children. These were for Head Start teachers or other preschool teachers. Sometimes I traveled to other communities to give the workshops. One year I worked full-time so my husband could stay home and dedicate himself to writing. That year I taught a morning preschool class for older four-year-olds. As at UM, I had lots of help and support from other staff, students, janitors, etc. The preschool program was very similar to the one I had just left at UT. However, the kindergarten lab at UM offered some specific teaching that would "help" the children adjust to first grade.

The teachers in the UM lab kindergarten had degrees in Elementary Education as well as having studied Child Development. The teachers taught the children how to move their chairs, how to get in line, and other practical things in preparation for first grade. The kindergarten teachers taught number concepts using

Graduate School, University Teaching, Parent Co-op, Head Start

Cuisenaire rods and they helped children advance in language skills by learning stories and memorizing poetry. There were also painting easels and creative art projects and puzzles, blocks, and house area and an outside playground. There were **opportunities to learn skills and to practice creative thinking** in this class. Helga McHugh's book, *Kindergarten, a Very Special Time and Place*, explained this program in detail. I thought these children were well prepared for first grade. It is true that they, just like the children at UT, came from families where the parents appreciated education and were willing to do what they thought would help in aiding their children's success in school.

It seemed to me in the late 1960s and early 1970s that preschool teachers were more interactive with the children than the preschool teachers in the lab at UT that I had observed ten years earlier. The head teachers of the programs at UM did not seem cautious and reserved. There were not many behavioral problems although I remember one little boy who would kick and start a fight in the four-year-old group. I think he was removed from the group for a rest when that happened, but I don't remember exactly the protocol for this. I was not the teacher in his class.

The year I had a class of older fours, I remember taking the children on a walk around the university area. At the outside of a building, one child noticed a large vending machine which had ice cream sandwiches in it. Immediately he said, "Let's get ice cream." The other children chanted, "We want ice cream." Of course there was no way I could buy all the children ice cream. In my mind I remembered the suggestion of when you can't give a child something in reality, maybe you can do it in imagination. So, let's pretend! I asked each child what kind they wanted, and I acted out handing it to them. "Now, be careful and don't let it drip on your clothes," I reminded them. They entered into the game with glee and pretended to eat and enjoy as we walked back to the classroom.

In Montana as I traveled around giving workshops and observing in Head Start rooms, I began to wonder if the model of the program that we had been using in the university lab schools was a good working model for other preschool programs. Often in those programs children did not attend school five days a week, nor did their home environment offer them a rich array of activities.

The concern for the welfare of all little children was becoming a national issue. This was evident to me when I attended the White House Conference on Children in 1970. In the conference hours, one of the groups I was in focused on the needs of the "economically poor" children. How can we best help children and families whose basic needs are not being met? This was a major concern and different groups proposed different solutions. At the conference I made some new friends who were also teaching in universities. In late hour confabs we shared the sorrows and joys of our personal lives and debated the relevance of what we were teaching in our university classes with the nitty-gritty of daily life.

Many other interesting things happened during my work at the University of Montana. I heard Jimmy Hymes speak. I heard Leland Jacobs tell a story and give a lecture. It was a story I had never liked. But in his telling, it was wonderful! I participated in a Bessell/Palomares workshop (see Part I, "Linda....") Colleagues shared in discussion about life and work and told me of books that I might find interesting such as *Room for One More*, *Masks of Sanity*, and *Oh, ye Jigs and Juleps*. In the stacks in the university library I happened upon *Visions of Order and Cradles of Eminence*. I ordered *Pathways to Madness* from a flyer I received about new books in family life studies.

Jess Lair from Montana State wrote *I Ain't Much Baby, but I'm all I've Got*. I liked it and I used it as corollary reading in some of my human development classes. I lectured and worked with students and graded a million papers. My graduate work that had been so steeped in research now was a great aid to me in critiquing text books and articles and in helping me to decide from time to time what I wanted to use in my own classes.

We changed our residence in Montana from the Clinton area to a ranch in the Bitterroot Valley. For me it was a new experience living on a real ranch. The much longer commute to get back and forth to work in Missoula was difficult. In these years in Montana, our children were growing up. It all seemed to happen too fast. Our lives were changing. We decided to move yet again...this time to Port Angeles, Washington, in 1976.

Graduate School, University Teaching, Parent Co-op, Head Start

PENINSULA COLLEGE PARENT CO-OP PRESCHOOL

My first job in Port Angeles was teaching a class for three-year-old children. In this setting the parents took turns as helpers in the classroom. The parents and I also met monthly with a parent co-coordinator/advisor who was sponsored by the college. The children came only two or three days a week. This was my first experience teaching a group that met less than five days a week. But the program itself was similar to those at UT and UM. We had choice/activity time with many creative activities, dramatic play, blocks, puzzles, books, etc. We had group time with finger plays, songs, and little games. It was harder to get to know the children than it had been in the five-days-a-week programs. I got to know the parents better than in the other programs due to their participation in the preschool class and in the monthly parent education meetings.

One thing I had not done before, which I found the children and I both enjoyed, was participating in making the snack. One of the parents working each day brought the ingredients for the healthy snack. Also, the parents helped in planning and carrying out activities, going on field trips, and cleaning up. The parents seemed to enjoy being a part of the program and knowing what was going on in a first-hand way. These parents were similar to the children's parents in the programs at UT and UM. By and large these people had been successful in school themselves and they were committed to spending energy and time in helping their children learn at each stage of development. I still know the families of some of my children in those classes. Most of those children have done well in school.

I was also hired about that time as a consultant through another university program to help students who were working on their child development associate degree. Most of these students were currently working as aides in Head Start programs and they wanted to get more education so they would be eligible for jobs with more responsibility and better salaries. The basic philosophy of how to teach young children and work with them was the same as I had been working under for fifteen years. I felt "at home" with guiding the students.

Sudie Doughton Mason

HEAD START TEACHER

My next employment was as a Head Start teacher for a group of children who were four years old. In this situation, each child was assessed as to their development in many different areas. We planned to help the children overcome any deficiencies so that they would succeed in kindergarten and in later schooling. Also, there was a many-pronged attack. We fed the children nutritious food, we worked with the parents, we had a nurse on staff, and other medical services available if needed.

We tried to provide a variety of activities in the classroom: creative activities, activities to promote social skills, stories, finger plays, songs, etc. We had specific activities for eye-hand coordination, activities for learning about patterns, activities for counting (three new emphases for me), and we had vigorous outside play. Sadly, the children only had regular class three mornings a week and sometimes they missed part of that. They might have to leave a class session for medical appointments. They might be absent due to missing the bus that came to pick them up at their homes. I thought that the children missed a lot when they missed even one day of school. One day each week we had a family program and the parents and siblings also came to school. The other day was for staff education and development.

One of the most interesting classroom projects one year was finding bones from some animal out on the playground. We kept adding to our collection. The children were intrigued by the bones. We discussed what animal it might be. We looked at the skeletons of various little animals. We talked about our bones too. At Halloween time the bones in the "skeleton" had new meaning for these children.

We were indeed more interactive with the children and more specific in some of our teaching than we had been back in the 1950s! But the teaching was not usually done individually or in a way in which it was easy to tell what each child understood and remembered from day to day. We did do some testing so we had an overall idea about what the children were learning.

There were many happy Head Start memories. Among them were: a wonderful storytelling workshop; a special Thanksgiving story about a turkey who tried to be the colors of many different

Graduate School, University Teaching, Parent Co-op, Head Start

animals; happiness in the faces of moms who got their first job primarily due to their participation in Head Start; a neat book showing how to make the paper bag puppets for all the folk tales; a workshop which taught us how to help children make up stories using their favorite animal as the focus.

I was saddened by the fact that our Head Start children sometimes had problems in kindergarten. Some repeated kindergarten. At times this would shock me, especially when it happened to a child I thought had made good progress during the Head Start year.

I believe that many children and their families profited a lot by their Head Start experience. The adults learned parenting skills, facts about good nutrition, and how to access social and medical programs that might be available to help them. Head Start made a positive influence in their lives, but I began to wonder what more could be done to help ensure school success. What could be done to help teachers plan programs that would meet the needs of each child so that they would be successfully engaged and learning every day—throughout their school years and throughout life?

Interestingly enough at this same time, I was being made acutely aware that it was not only children from "the other side of the track" that "fail" in school. I'm sure I had known that all my life, but often it is only when we face something personally that the impact of it is truly felt and known. There were some children in my own family having trouble in school. I also had friends who were "very well educated" and some of their children were having problems. It seemed we were missing the boat with a lot of kids. My teaching career was soon to take a different road in my own search for what might help.

Part VI
Montessori Work

Dedication: For **Betty Nicholson**,
              my mentor, my co-worker, my friend

Betty Watson Nicholson has a master's degree in elementary education from Pennsylvania State College (now Pennsylvania State University). She has taught in schools in the states and also in oil camps overseas for the English-speaking children. These schools were located in Venezuela, Peru, Saudi Arabia, and Indonesia.

Her Montessori certification is from the St. Nicholas Training Centre in London. In 1979, she began the Montessori Community School in Sequim, Washington. She moved the school to Port Angeles in 1980 with the help of her husband, Lorne Nicholson. He was always very interested and supportive of the school. He served as treasurer until his death in 1985.

Now that Betty is retired she is active in many community and church activities. A special joy for her is spending time with her three children and four grandchildren.

Sudie Doughton Mason

Betty's quiet genius was evident to me in my first observations of her class in the early 1980s. The children seemed to have confidence and a great presence in the room, yet they worked calmly. They concentrated on first one activity and then another. Their abilities and attitudes amazed me. I went back often to observe. I noticed that Betty had a way of working with children that always helped the child make that little jump up to the next level of understanding. Even in her show-and-tell sessions she found ways to prompt the children to express themselves and tell unusual and interesting things.

After I began teaching with her, I realized that Betty was very focused on keeping the school in a workable format financially and in all ways. She was careful not to overextend the program. In this day and age administrators often seem to introduce one program on top of another and expect teachers to fit it all in. I think Betty's idea of figuring out a main plan that was successful and workable, and staying with it, was a good one.

Betty believed that our school should try to keep the tuition as low as possible so that many families could afford the program. She and Loren had bought usable tables and chairs at school sales for old equipment. She had made much of her Montessori equipment. She combined her interest in economy, garage sales, and teaching. She picked up papers for art work, puzzles, and a lot of good books at 25 cents apiece. These books were to have on hand for the children who had finished our phonics program and were now independent readers.

What I appreciate most from our long teaching association was her consistency in doing what she set out to do, which was to see that each child was learning and progressing. She did well what Montessori had emphasized, in the sense of letting the "child increase and the teacher decrease." She never made her own personal interests or personality the focus. She was truly "present" for the long haul and the daily work with every child she taught.

Foreword

Montessori education is "in the news" lately due to the fact that it has been exactly one hundred years since Dr. Maria Montessori opened her first school in a slum in Rome, Italy.

Montessori Work

(Jeffrey MacDonald, "Montessori Looks Back – and Ahead", *USA Today*, Jan 26, 2007.) This year there will be a traveling exhibit to celebrate her contributions, and there will be various conferences highlighting Dr. Montessori's educational method, according to this article. What a surprise when Mike Doherty, a parent of three of our alums, knocked on my kitchen door recently and handed me this newspaper clipping!

In preparation for editing this part of my book, I have read again some of Montessori's own writings. I was impressed by many things. She credited the work of Itard and Seguin as being very important in the development of her philosophy and methods. Montessori describes translating the works of Itard and Seguin into Italian and writing it out in long hand in order to "weigh the meaning of their words and absorb the spirit of the authors." (*The Discovery of the Child*, page 30.) It seems to me that that was a mighty achievement. Other educators and psychologists that she felt influenced her are also mentioned in Chapter 2 in *The Discovery of the Child*. Montessori developed her methods from combining ideas and discoveries of others with what she herself discovered was successful in her work with children. She made some changes in what she considered the best methods as she went along.

In our school, Betty and I based what we were doing on our comprehensive study of the Montessori Method. Most of all we tried to "absorb the spirit of her teaching" and let it shine through our own. We followed her basic philosophy and teaching principles and used many of the Montessori materials. However, we did use some of our own ideas, some of the things we had learned in other programs, and we made changes from time to time.

Montessori teachers may find the information in this section more interesting and understandable than other people will. I encourage all people who are seeking good ways to teach young children to take the time and effort to visit Montessori schools, read Montessori's books, and also books other people have written about her work. Information is also available on the web about various training programs for people who want to become Montessori teachers.

This section of my book is a discussion about some of the ways that Betty and I taught in our school in the years that we were the only teachers there. Hopefully it will stimulate thoughts and discussion for parents and teachers who read this section. It does not include detailed information on how to use all the Montessori materials. It is not meant in any way to serve as a guide for a person who wants to become a Montessori teacher. That individual needs a comprehensive course in Montessori education. **There is no shortcut.**

This section of my book will include four parts:
- Our training to be Montessori teachers
- Introduction to our school, Montessori Community School ... as told by The School
- Questions I was frequently asked
- More information on various aspects of our teaching and program

Note: Montessori called the teachers "directors" instead of "teachers." Betty and I never followed that tradition and we were known as teachers. I use the word "teacher" rather than "directors" in my writing about our work. To simplify, I also use initials M.M. frequently instead of writing out Maria Montessori or the Montessori Method.

OUR TRAINING TO BE MONTESSORI TEACHERS

Our certifications in the Montessori Method were earned through the St. Nicholas Training Centre for the Montessori Method of Education in London, England. Betty had completed her course about ten years before I did mine. Her course was designated for working with children three through eight years old. I believe her workshop instructor had actually worked with Maria Montessori. I enrolled in a similar correspondence course with St. Nicholas but my course only covered the work with the child from three through five. For the purposes of this section I will describe what my work was like.

The correspondence part of the training was organized with a comprehensive text book. Each student had a tutor that worked with him or her throughout the correspondence study. My tutor took the time to comment on my answers to questions, and she noted things I needed to reread and think about. She seemed to be very experienced and knowledgeable. I liked the fact that she was also interested in me personally, my past experiences and the surroundings in which I studied and wrote, sometimes from our fishing boat! She circled my misspellings in red pencil. There was no computer in the early '80s to spell check for me! Once I had to redo a lesson before I could proceed. I appreciated the time and energy she spent in trying to help me understand each lesson. The correspondence part took me about a year to complete.

As a part of my study I read M.M.'s books: *The Discovery of the Child, The Secret of Childhood,* and *The Absorbent Mind.* It became evident to me that it was very important to understand Montessori's philosophy and the discoveries she had made about children in order to fully comprehend the various layers of meaning in the activities and methods.

I observed three or four Montessori classrooms as a part of my study. Each school seemed to be a **variation** on the **same theme.** I liked the fact that each was a little different. They ranged from somewhat orderly to very orderly; from not very calm and quiet to very calm and quiet; from having a lot of Montessori equipment being used to having some Montessori equipment being used, etc. There were differences in the number of children in a group, in the amount of creative art materials available, and the personality of the teachers, yet there was no mistaking that each of these schools was a Montessori School. In each I saw adults observing children and giving demonstrations to children. I saw teachers who were dignified and focused. I saw young children working with concentration for fairly long periods of time. I also saw some interesting "teacher-made" activities that were being used following some of Montessori's teaching principles. The teachers in these schools had come from a variety of training programs. One of the teachers had a St. Nicholas certificate; in another school, the teacher's certification was AMI, Association Montessori Internationale. I do not remember about the training that the teachers in the other schools had completed.

In the summer of 1984, I attended a two-week St. Nicholas-sponsored workshop in Santa Rosa, California. I took with me a notebook of various Practical Life Activities that I had developed for teaching. I also took with me pictures of some "Sensorial Materials" that Bill and I had made.

The leaders of the workshop demonstrated to us the use of all the general Montessori materials for young children. After seeing how the workshop leaders did them, we practiced giving the demonstrations to other students (acting as children) while the instructors watched and later critiqued our work.

The successful completion of a long, comprehensive exam was the last requirement in the course. I was proud as a peacock when my certification paper arrived later that fall. I felt like "Wow, now this is mine, I understand, I have learned, I can do it!"

However, I was quite chagrined soon after that. While working and constantly observing Betty, I realized that I was still learning new things. What? After all that work, there was more to learn? Papa would have smiled and said, "Of course, did you really think anybody ever knows it all?"

Over the years, my training was furthered by opportunities to observe teachers and Montessori schools other than the ones I had seen earlier and reported on to my tutor. We also had other Montessori teachers, some Saint Nicholas trained and some from other traditions, who came and worked with us at our school. I attended a conference on using Whole Language in Montessori Schools. I read more books and manuals and educational publications from a wide variety of sources. We made a few changes through the years. These may be reflected in my overall comments. However, **I tried to remember and discuss the main parts of our program from the years that Betty and I taught together. I thought this would simplify and limit the discussion, yet it would include the elements I believe were most important about our work.**

MONTESSORI COMMUNITY SCHOOL
From the Point of View of "The School" (circa 1987)

I am the school that Betty and Sudie had many years ago. I wish you could have been there and seen and heard all the things I experienced for many, many years. The children played, the children worked, the children learned. My, how they did learn!

The children arrived each morning at nine. After hanging up

Montessori Work

their coats, the children looked around the room, usually spoke to several friends, and then chose an activity to begin their day. I had two lovely, big rooms with wonderful activities. There were puzzles, games, and books. There were creative art materials: an easel for painting, paper and crayons, etc. The practical life activities included flower arranging, washing the tables and the easel, buttoning, zipping, pouring from a pitcher, etc. There were Montessori Sensorial and Math and Language materials. There really weren't many rules to follow; just talk quietly with your friends, put your activity away, and clean up your work area before choosing something else. Oh, yes, there were two more rules: come straight back to the room after going to the bathroom, and don't interrupt someone else's lesson with the teacher.

The whole idea was for the children to come when they were three or four years old and stay for their kindergarten year too. That way they had a chance to really use and eventually master many of the activities we had to offer. Everybody belonged to a big class with twenty-three other children and two teachers for most of the day. The final forty-five minutes were spent in a smaller group. Sudie had the younger children and Betty had the older ones.

I loved to watch all the children. I remember some of them especially. There was the little boy who had trouble seeing but with all those tactile Montessori activities he learned the shapes and how to sort and match many things. Later with the tactile numbers, he learned their forms from feeling them and he learned their names. Soon he could write the numbers too. With the tactile letters he had no trouble learning their shapes and sounds. Sudie wrote out the words to his first book in a large print that was about double the size of the printing in the book. He put his eyes close to the page and he read. Soon he learned to read the print in the books!

One year Betty had two kids who wrote numbers from 1 to beyond 2,000! Of course the children had worked on this daily for many months. They had used the sheets of paper with one hundred squares and then scotch-taped them all together and then rolled them up in a big roll. What a splash it made when the children would let that roll drop and we could see all those numbers!

At music time, there were often children who could carry a tune better than Betty or Sudie could, so it was really funny when one would say, "Just a minute, I think that tune goes more like this...." Once when the teachers were trying to play some song on a xylophone, a little girl offered to take over and she played it much better!

Another year a mother brought a tent that would hold two children. Two kids at a time would get in the tent with a book and read it, saying the words in unison, with enthusiasm and delight. Sometimes a five-year-old would read to a younger child.

I thought it was amazing that nearly all the children who were with us at least two years (if it included the kindergarten year) learned to read and to recognize and understand basic numbers and write them to one hundred. Some children like the ones mentioned above developed advanced skills in areas of their interests. How could so much happen? I began to observe more carefully. I don't understand it all, but I'm going to tell you about some of the things that I think influenced the children's success.

THE TEN-MINUTE DAILY INDIVIDUAL LESSONS (BETTY'S ADAPTATION OF M.M.'S LESSONS)

During the two-and-a-quarter-hour activity time each day, Betty and Sudie sat at their little tables and worked with each of their twelve children, one at a time for about ten minutes each. I remember hearing Betty say that she came up with this plan because in other methods that she had used it seemed like some of the children took up more than their fair share of time. With this method each child had daily, individual attention from the teacher. **How great for the child to have special time with the teacher for learning at his or her own rate.** The lesson of each day depended on what the child had done the day before. (In some schools the only time a child is seen individually by an adult is when he or she has misbehaved or "not learned" in another setting.

A LONG CHOICE/ACTIVITY TIME

I mean it was really a long time—if you took out the time for the individual lesson each child still had over two hours a day for choice/activity time. We had lots of Montessori materials available and also many general preschool activities. We wanted the children to have ample opportunity to do a wide variety of things and time to move through their work cycle doing easy, hard, and harder activities, and observing others. Many of the Montessori activities in the room had initial exercises that were simple, but there were also more complex ways to use the same equipment when the child was ready for it. Children naturally saw equipment and activities being used at a more elementary level or a more advanced level than their own.

The children seemed to enjoy the process of working, as well as seeing the completion of an activity. Children were free to work at a table, on the floor, observe others, and go to the bathroom when they needed to. The teacher was aware of the pattern of activity of each child in the room, as she could glance up easily from her table and see the whole room. Of course, when it was needed, she could go and help someone or send an older child to help a younger one.

A RELATIVELY CALM ATMOSPHERE

The teachers and children spoke in moderately low voices during activity time. Visual as well as auditory distractions were kept to a minimum. The placement and type of materials available lent themselves to fairly orderly, purposeful activity most of the time. Children were not easily distracted by others. General rules, such as the child who took out the material could use it as long as he liked, helped to keep arguments from occurring. At the beginning of school in the fall, the return of students from the year before was very instrumental in helping the new students learn to work and play in the environment.

TEACHERS WERE INTENT ON PRESENTING SPECIFIC INFORMATION DAILY

The teachers made teaching the first priority. Because the children were successful at **tasks that were very easy to hear or see, teaching had its own intrinsic rewards.** The same general program was used year after year as were the same teaching materials and the same series of books. One parent asked Sudie one time if she didn't get bored hearing the same stories over and over. Her answer was, "No, because I'm not listening to the story so much as listening to all the nuances in the child's reading."

The teachers could focus on teaching because they did not have to keep many written records or give tests or invent new things to do each day. They did not, after the children's initial adjustment time, have any major behavioral problems to deal with. They prepared only a simple snack for each day. May, the last month of school, was always a busier time than usual...with year books to put together and having parent-teacher conferences, but somehow Betty and Sudie kept teaching up until the last day of school.

GOOD HEALTH AND GOOD ATTENDANCE

Our children missed very little school. They arrived eager to start the day. I know that in some other schools children with bad attendance may be smart enough to catch up easily and some children, even with good attendance, don't progress as they should. But in our school attendance mattered a lot, because your lesson/work was based on what you had done at your last lesson and if your last lesson was yesterday, it was easier to remember what you had learned. The teachers likewise had good attendance and remembered what the child had done the day before.

THIRTY-MINUTE GROUP TIME WITH TEACHER

Each day the children had group activities led by teacher who gave them their individual lessons. Group time provided many opportunities for the child to learn to listen, to speak, and to participate in a group.

The group time was a **contrast** to the activity time and also to the child's experience in the individual lesson. The group time was interesting and fun for the teachers as well as for the children. We generally kept the same weekly schedule. But even with the different focus each day, the teacher had time to add finger plays, an active song or two, some number work, maybe a game like catching the ball or walking the line. Of course, Betty and Sudie, as experienced teachers, had a long repertoire of games, poems, songs, stories, etc. they could spontaneously "pull out of the hat" when needed. Some of those were a riot!

Activities for group time according to the day of the week...
Monday: Show and Tell
Tuesday: Stories
Wednesday: Crafts
Thursday: Science, geography, or art history lesson
Friday: Music (generally singing songs with all twenty-four children together)

I'm not sure what my favorite day of the year was. It was probably one of the holiday celebration days when everyone had special snacks together, the parents came to help, and the ordinary group activity for that day was superseded by great holiday hoopla. Wow, it's hard to say! The everyday joy of watching children learn and practice what they learned was hard to beat.
The End of the story from the school's point of view!

QUESTIONS I WAS OFTEN ASKED

WHY DID BETTY'S SCHOOL APPEAL TO YOU?
- It first appealed to me because I could see such vitality in the life of the children in the room. I could see a lot of **initiative** being taken by the children. I observed children **working independently**. I could see children **helping others** and **handling problems**. I had been involved in evaluation of some preschool programs earlier in my career, in which we were observing for children's growth in some of these same areas. In Betty's preschool and kindergarten, which used essentially a different program from the ones I had been critiquing, the children abounded in these sought after characteristics.
- Most of the children were actively engaged in work or play in a generally calm and thoughtful way.
- Another reason I liked it was the simplicity of furnishings and layout. Betty had bought secondhand tables and chairs. She had made many of her materials as I mentioned earlier. All of the emphasis in her class was about what the children were learning and doing, not on fancy equipment. My own upbringing had been similar. At home we did not have all the latest toys and the

nicest "stuff;" but our parents talked with us, told us stories, and helped us individually and expected us to be thoughtful in our use of materials and in our play with other children.

- I also liked the multi-age group. I had not seen a multi-age group since my days in the day care center in Chile. A multi-age group of young children seems like a more natural grouping to me than having children all the same age. The older children can help with the younger ones and any particular needs of any one age group are not so overwhelming because everyone is not in that same stage. This also was important in helping to maintain the calm atmosphere spoken of earlier.

AFTER SEVERAL YEARS IN THE PROGRAM, DID YOU OBSERVE OTHER THINGS THAT YOU ESPECIALLY LIKED?

- Yes, I noticed that a shy child was not overwhelmed by other children in this setting. They seemed to talk fairly easily with children sitting or working close to them after a few weeks of initial adjustment. One or two children could not easily dominate the whole group. Children who were originally loud and boisterous calmed down.
- Having children of various ages and teachers who encouraged each child to feel successful working at their own level seemed to foster security, progress, and an interest in each other's work, and occasionally playful competition among friends. Children sometimes spontaneously complimented each other.
- If a child stayed in the program three years, he or she had the experience of being one of the younger children, one of the middle, and then one of the older children. Even the children who were only there two years benefited from being among the younger and among the older children. In many programs where each child changes to a completely new room each year, the child's birthday has determined that he or she is always in the same relationship by age to most of the other children.
- By spending time each day with each child in the lesson, we could see needs or special talents or interests that each child had. This knowledge was helpful not only at the lesson time, but also in knowing what kinds of activities to encourage the child to

do during the major work/play session or in interacting with the child at group time.

- I liked the fact that the children had such a long choice/activity time each day and that the basic activities were the same from day to day. With the long choice time, most children who wanted to use a certain activity would get to use it that day. If not, it would be available the next day and for many days to come.
- The children's choices of activities often reflected an ongoing interest and increasing skills rather than just the initial attractiveness of the activity.
- The children seemed very engaged in every aspect of the day: their little lessons, the activities at choice time, snack, and the group time after snack. These children seemed to me to enjoy work and play. They also seemed able to express many of their own ideas and to have an influence on each other and also on our program as it progressed from day to day.

WHY DID PARENTS WANT THEIR CHILDREN IN MONTESSORI COMMUNITY SCHOOL?

- Sometimes parents had good experiences with Montessori schools before coming to Port Angeles. They knew some of the benefits of the program, e.g., the "sensorial" and math materials that help give children a great foundation for math and science.
- Sometimes the parents wanted their child to have a strong phonics background for reading. Betty emphasized the reading program and the "word was out" that her children learned to read!
- One parent told me she could tell it was a good school because no one was crying when the parents came to pick up the children. This might not have been the original reason for sending the child, however.
- Another parent told me one of the things she liked was that the children learned how to stay busy with activities without having to be entertained by someone else. She saw a carry-over in this at home.
- Probably in many instances the parents knew other families that had liked our program; it was for that reason that they ventured to send their child.

- A few of our parents had bad memories of their own years in school. These people were consciously searching for a different preschool environment from the one they had as a child, one that might help their child be more successful in school than they had been.

HOW WERE THE MONTESSORI MATERIALS AND ACTIVITIES DIFFERENT FROM THE GENERAL ACTIVITIES AVAILABLE IN MOST OTHER PRESCHOOLS?

- With the practical life materials, the differences were more in how the materials were organized and presented to the child than in the objects themselves. For instance, we had a little broom and dustpan and dusting cloths. We had sponges and buckets for table washing and easel clean-up. However, children usually helped with the real cleaning, rather than in "play cleaning." We gave little demonstrations on how to do these things.

- All the Montessori activities had a preparation part, a "doing" part, and a clean-up/put-away part. In most preschools I had worked in previously, the children all cleaned up together with the teacher's help at the end of the activity time. I thought the emphases on the three parts of an activity as mentioned above worked so well that I tried to be sure all our activities included those emphases. Each child finished and put up the activity he or she had taken down. He/she did not pass it on to another child. If a child did a puzzle, he/she had to check to be sure all the pieces were in place. If the child had lost a piece, he/she looked for it immediately and usually it was easy to find at that point. Then the puzzle went back to the shelf.

- To me the most striking differences in the Montessori materials were in **the design and fabrication** of many of the "**sensorial materials**" (*The Discovery of the Child*, pp. 99-105). Montessori developed these to help train children to use their senses acutely, and learn and remember. These materials emphasized and isolated certain qualities of the objects, making it easier for a child to distinguish those qualities. For instance, if the child was learning shapes, the material used had all the shapes painted the same color and made about the same size, so each shape varied from the other in one aspect only, its conformation.

Montessori Work

- We made many of our materials. I had not done that in my other preschool work. Betty had made her fastening frames, a set of long rods, the brown stair, and the pink tower. I made a set of color tablets (Montessori, *The Discovery of the Child*, pp.128, 129). I was able to get the color chips from a paint company and I mounted them on black tag board. They were pretty worn out after fifteen years of use! Betty had bought many sensorial materials that needed extra precision, such as the knobbed cylinders and the geometric cabinet.
- Montessori herself (*The Discovery of the Child*, pp.128, 129) used little tablets with silk threads to teach children about colors. In one advanced activity, she had nine colors and each color was presented in seven shades from light to dark. The children learned first to grade three shades of one color from light to dark; then maybe five of them; and finally all seven. I bought a lovely set of these sixty-three tablets that had been hand-painted by a Montessori teacher in Oregon. Once, several of my five-year-olds worked on this activity together and made a giant sun with nine rays, one of each color, and the tablets were graded from the darkest to the lightest in each ray. It was lovely.
- The arithmetic and reading materials were developed in a way to make it possible for the child to learn simple things, one at a time, and then to practice using the materials. Learning proceeded in a slow and sequential fashion.
- Our activities also differed from most preschools in that we consciously tried to limit the materials and activities made from plastic. We made an effort to provide lovely containers that would provide visual and tactile stimuli to the child. We used baskets, wood trays, metal trays, mats of different material to work on, etc. For several years we used little glass punch cups for our juice at snack time. When these were washed they sparkled and any debris on the cup was immediately seen by the child and could be washed away!

Notes and Comments

Montessori's book, *The Discovery of the Child*, explains in detail more about her philosophy, the materials, and their use.

Understanding Montessori's philosophy is important in making the proper use of the materials as I have discussed earlier. Each activity is a part of the comprehensive program of education.

In retrospect, I remember the "three parts of a task" were also important in home management classes I had in college. It is interesting that in the home management classes we also learned how to give demonstrations. I never learned if Montessori and home management might have had some "common ancestor," but it seemed a distinct possibility.

Some of the items sold to parents and preschools are similar to some of the Montessori materials mentioned above, but they are not as useful and helpful as they might be due to the fact that the manufacturers seem to insist on making everything in a variety of colors. As a result, the different sizes of boxes or cups made to fit inside each other or to be placed on top of each other from largest to smallest vary by color as well as size. That makes it harder for the child to focus on the difference in the size of each box or cup. The size is the important aspect of the objects in this instance.

WAS IT HARD TO ACCEPT THE IDEA OF TEACHING NUMBERS, LETTERS, READING, AND WRITING TO PRESCHOOL AND KINDERGARTEN AGE CHILDREN?

- Yes, for me it was. If anybody had asked me about teaching these subjects to preschoolers in the first half of my career, I would have said, "Little children need to spend time playing and learning in a stimulating environment. They will be picking up lots of general knowledge in a non-threatening way. They can learn the three R's in regular school."
- My reasons for feeling this way were not only because I thought children should be busy with other things, but because I thought most methods to teach letters and numbers did not suit little children's learning styles. I was afraid that early failure would take its toll. In most of the methods I was familiar with in the 1960s, **there was a lot of seat work, a lot of time with the teacher talking to the group, a lot of teaching from a visual or auditory aspect only, and lack of daily knowledge of what each child understood about the numbers or letters.** This would not be good for preschool children.

Montessori Work

- I wondered at first about what I saw in Betty's classroom. It was the same kind of quandary I felt when I first saw the children in Chile put on such polished holiday programs. It went against what I had learned in college. (In Section III, I explain how my feelings about it all changed after I saw Sra. Haydee working with the children, practicing with them daily, and helping them to gain skill and confidence, etc.) In this situation, when I saw how Betty's children were learning numbers and letters with the daily practices which seemed interesting to the children, many of my assumptions changed about what was good or bad. I also had the opportunity to discuss what I was observing with Betty and with my tutor in the correspondence course.
- The foundational work that Betty's children had accomplished with practical life and sensorial materials before the introduction of numbers and letters had prepared the way for learning numbers and letters. Those earlier activities involved the use of many senses and especially of the hands for feeling and developing some sort of "motor memory." They helped the children learn to follow procedures, concentrate, notice details, develop memory, etc.
- The use of the children's hands in learning was continued as the children progressed to more advanced subjects such as the numbers. The teaching of number concepts, symbols, and, later, the letter sounds were all done slowly and carefully with tactile materials. Because the teacher worked with each child individually and checked to see what the child remembered (part three of the III period lesson), she knew what the child had learned each day and often it was evident to the child also. She backed up if necessary. All of this helped to reduce the chance of early failure.
- I learned to love teaching numbers and letters to young children following the Montessori procedures and materials. Children seemed to have a natural affinity for the methods. Most four-year-olds were eager to begin learning numbers after their mastery of many practical life and sensorial materials. Also, the children who came to us just for their kindergarten year learned rapidly with these methods.

IN YOUR SCHOOL, WHAT FORM OF PUNISHMENT FOR BAD BEHAVIOR DID YOU USE?

- We did not have much bad behavior. If there was a problem, we would have the child sit at our table for a while, losing the freedom to work as he chose, yet he could watch another child's lesson or just rest. The length of time was "up to the teacher." After a few minutes, when it was convenient for the teacher, she would talk briefly with the child if she felt it necessary. If the child had calmed down and was ready to work or play appropriately, the teacher would allow the child to go back to the activities and find something to do. I think giving the child time to rest and calm down was a good plan. The child did not receive much attention as an outcome of improper behavior.

- Many things helped keep the problems or the need for intervention at a minimum. Some of these were: keeping the talking level in the room fairly low, having lots of interesting things to do, having general rules about the use of the activities, having children of varied ages. Also the fact that each year we had returning children who knew the routine and expectations was very important. They were good mentors for the new children.

- Sometimes in the beginning of a year a young child might act in some "naughty" way and we would try to have a low-key approach by discussing it briefly with the child and redirecting the child to a different activity. However, hitting, spitting, cussing, destroying someone else's project were all behaviors that were stopped immediately by removing the child from the activity and having him/her come to sit near the teacher. The same procedure was followed as outlined in the first paragraph.

- Once, early in the school year, I had a child who was hitting other children; I seemed to be getting nowhere with him by removing him from activities and having him sit beside me. The hitting frequently reoccurred on the next day. After school one day, I discussed the situation with Betty. I thought maybe we could not keep this child in the school. Betty offered to take charge of him, do his lessons, monitor his behavior, etc. I gladly turned him over to her. In the beginning she had him do his activities quietly at her table while she gave lessons. Soon, she could allow him to be move around the room like the other children. He did not ever hit or hurt another child at our school. I relate this happening to point out that one teacher may be a lot better with a child than another teacher. The teacher's demeanor, personality, and sense of authority add another dimension to any technique. Betty told me once something to the effect that the child must always know that the teacher is in charge and not doubt it. She added, "However, the goal is that the child will learn to feel that we are all on the same team." I think with difficult children she succeeded better than I did.

Comments and Thoughts

I think having the child sit by the teacher or near her might have had many long-lasting benefits. The child would not feel as banished as he or she might in a time-out chair in a corner. The child understood that it was the teacher's call as to when he/she returned to the activities. The child would "sense" the teacher's authority (in most instances) and be learning to judge the nuances of her facial expressions. This was a subjective situation, not objective. Having a relationship with the teacher and feeling a sense of her authority as well as her care is crucial. (See Part II, "Good Authority.")

Betty tells the story of a five-year-old student in her class who went home and told her mother, "That teacher thinks she can tell me what to do."

Accordingly, the mother responded, "That teacher is right, she **can** tell you what to do!"

DID YOU FIND THE CHILDREN WERE LESS CREATIVE IN THE ORDERLY MONTESSORI ENVIRONMENT THAN THEY WERE IN THE OTHER PRESCHOOLS?

- No, in fact, the children in our school were in general more creative in their art, and in their questions and ideas, than most of the children I had worked with in other settings. Our Montessori children painted, drew, cut out and pasted using their own ideas. They thought of different ways of doing things, they decorated their projects with original ideas, they thought of new words for songs, ways to solve problems, etc. They even had suggestions for how to improve things.

- Their creativity may have been fostered by a certain degree of order. Time is not lost hunting for materials; the child knows the routine and in our situation the children had plenty of time to work without feeling rushed. The children did not constantly have to adjust to a new structure, different adults or different activities.
- The multi-age group may have also indirectly influenced their creativity. Due to the variety in ages, experiences, interest, and talent, there was a great variation in the art work of the children. This may have helped the children be more open to experimentation and less critical of each other.
- Maybe being in the same school with the same teachers and classmates and many of the same projects and activities available for two or three years "aided and abetted" creativity. But that same factor might have been detrimental if the teachers did not like and encourage creativity in appropriate situations.
- I do believe that in many instances how adults feel about children's creativity will influence how creative the children are. Most of the parents appreciated the children's creative art work. Some of our children had been in pre-three programs which had emphasized creative activities.
- Betty and I greatly valued the children's creativity. I had studied Lowenfeld's ideas in graduate school and I had used his book *Creative and Mental Growth* as a text when I taught courses on children's art. Betty had actually had Lowenfeld as a professor when she was in college. I imagine partially due to his influence, we both understood the great value of children's creative expression in art and we were aware that it represented more than what can be seen just looking at the final product.
- We distinguished between three types of activities: 1. Those that were primarily follow-the-instruction type; 2. Creative activities a child could "do their own way;" 3. Work that was a combination of a follow-the-instruction and then add your own decorations. (Crafts are an example of the last type.) See the discussion on the difference in skill-based activities and creative ones in Part II of this book for more information on my ideas. For more on children's art, refer to some of the books on art listed in the Bibliography.
- One thought occurs to me now. Most of the activities in our Montessori room did not have as a main emphasis the expression of a child's personal emotions and ideas. Activities that explicitly

emphasized that expression may have had a special appeal both to the children and the teachers—maybe more so than in other preschool environments that have many types of "creative activities." That would be an interesting question to research. (It may have something to do with the value of contrast which I have mentioned previously.)

- Looking back at the question, I think our school was not overly orderly at all. I think we were "just right" in the amount of order we kept in general in the classroom. Now the closet was another matter...it probably reflected our inborn tendency to chaos. But we kept that closet door shut during class. And remember, the order was not just the teachers' responsibility. The children helped us keep the classroom in order.

DID THE CHILDREN RESENT NOT BEING ABLE TO DO THE MONTESSORI ACTIVITIES UNTIL THEY HAD A DEMONSTRATION?

- I was surprised that this never seemed to bother anybody. Of course, we had lots of regular activities that did not require a demonstration so there were plenty of things to do. I often have wondered why the children so well accepted the rule about the Montessori activities. Maybe it was because they were not toys and the children understood this at some level. Also, there is some protection in the system because you are not always getting into things that you can't do and possibly feeling discouraged as a result.

- As teachers, we tried to observe the children's progress and pick up on any particular interests. We would introduce an activity to a child when we observed an interest and also thought he or she would be capable of completing the activity successfully. Maybe the children recognized that this was happening in the classroom and they knew their turn would come.

- There were rare occasions when a child took down a complicated piece of equipment that he or she had not had a demonstration on. Although we had these general rules and expectations, it was not considered a discipline matter if the child forgot and took out something he/she had not been introduced to. We treated it in a low-key way.

- One child I saw do this was a three-year-old girl who took apart the trinomial cube, a complex piece of equipment. She put it back together by herself without any visible plan and with little effort. I recognized her talent, readiness, and interest. The next day I gave her a lesson. In the lesson/demonstration it was easy to see the relationships between the prisms in each layer and this was one of the points to the exercise. It was always a joy to watch this child work with the trinomial cube, which she continued to take out and work with frequently. I never saw another child do this work so easily.

WERE THE CHILDREN WHO STAYED FOR THE KINDERGARTEN YEAR WITH YOU BORED WHEN THEY WENT TO FIRST GRADE SINCE THEY ALREADY KNEW HOW TO READ?

- I don't think so. I never heard parents or teachers complain much about this. Maybe it was because most of the children could work independently. The teachers could give the children books or things to work on that would interest them. In many first-grade classes there were other children (not from our school) who could also read.
- I remember hearing Betty talk with some parents who questioned her about this as a possible future problem. She told them that usually the children were not bored at all in school as there would be so many new things for them to learn about and adjust to. And also if the school work was not too difficult, it was a good time for the parents to have their child take special music lessons or get involved with sports or scouts or something else in the community that would challenge them.
- We tried to emphasize with our children the on-going nature of education and the wonder it can bring to life and also their own responsibility to keep education interesting. Sometimes a child would come up to me and announce that she/he was "bored." I always tried to accept the statement nonchalantly and to also remind the child that here the children didn't have to work or play intensely all the time. It was okay to rest a little, or watch someone else, and choose an activity when ready. I resisted the temptation to "solve the problem" for the child. Most of our children caught

the ball, so to speak, and took charge of their own play and work at activity time. So hopefully they continued to take charge of much of their own learning for the rest of their lives!

Comments

My friend Linda Pisciotta, who is the mother of Elizabeth, (a student I had twenty years ago who is now in a Ph.D. program) called to relay this message. "Elizabeth says to tell you that she is still using her Montessori training. Just the other night she was getting bored with a project and suddenly remembered what she learned as a preschooler**…it is my responsibility to figure out a way to keep my education interesting!**"

WHAT ABOUT THE SOCIAL DEVELOPMENT OF THE CHILDREN?

- The children had opportunity to develop friendships while at school. Children often sat together and talked with each other while they were working on their numbers or drawing pictures. I remember two little girls who loved to sit together and draw princesses.
- Three-year-olds often enjoyed playing with a box of little blocks I had. There were also little animals in the box and a few trees. They could play with these in a defined area. The play had to be relatively quiet so that the children around them could continue in their work without undue noise and interruption.
- Snack time also offered a chance to talk and interact with others.
- The little group games we played I think benefited the children socially.
- Also, the Montessori Practical Life activities that helped the children learn manners were important.
- The Bessell/Palomares activities that I used from time to time helped children learn more about each other, which would directly or indirectly affect their social lives. (See information in paper on "Linda" in Part I.)
- Betty and I recognized that children needed opportunities to play with other children in ways that were not available in our school. We tried to remind parents of this and of the fact that we

did not have dramatic house play, or a place for building large structures with unit blocks, or an outside playground. Parents often arranged to have a friend come home to play after school. Some children attended day care centers after school and had an opportunity to play there

Comments

Probably there were families that did not bring their children to our school because they thought their children needed a preschool with more opportunity to "play" than we offered. And it could be that some children did need that. Hopefully those parents were also providing means for teaching the children manners and providing opportunities for their child to work with activities that would promote the development of attention, concentration, and memory.

We did not try to meet all the needs of the children. (See the next question and answer for more thoughts about this.) The children were in our school only three hours a day. Parents, the extended family, the community, and the churches would all need to do their part. I do think that the overall development of confidence and the progress in general learning at our school had both direct and indirect positive influences on children's relationships with others.

HOW DID YOU MANAGE TO KEEP "BURNOUT" AT BAY?

- I think because of all the things we did **not** do, and our conscious effort to keep our program focused on the main things we were trying to accomplish, we were not overwhelmed. We did not get "burned out." Of course, there were some days that were more difficult than others, but in general we felt a sense of satisfaction because of the everyday progress we observed and the good times we had with the children.
- Getting out the paints for the easel, cutting the newsprint for painting, and putting out paper for other projects was about the extent of the daily preparation for the art activities. We did not as a rule use photocopied materials or printed forms except for paper printed in squares for the number writing. Sometimes colored pencils had to be sharpened. I came to work an hour

early and kept a few children during that time whose parents had to be at work around eight. The children helped me get ready. Sometimes we were able to complete several individual lessons before everyone else arrived.

- There did not seem to be as much clean-up as I had experienced in some of the other preschools I had taught in. Some of this was because the children cleaned up as they went along, and they also helped at the general clean-up before snacks.
- We just did each day's work as it came. The work in the lessons was built on what the child had accomplished the day before as stated earlier.
- All the teaching materials were readily at hand.
- We did not ordinarily have to keep many written records, just a few notes.
- Major paper supplies were bought only once or twice a year and they were easily available in our closets or other storage spaces. Paints, crayons, pencils, craft materials were bought once a year. Sometimes we had to go out and hunt for stickers for the calendar project.
- Formal staff meetings were minimal compared to other settings I was familiar with; possibly this was because there were only two of us and we were able to check with each other at the end of each day if there was anything that needed discussing. We had divided up who was in charge of what. For example, Betty planned the craft, I took charge of music. We each were in charge of the activities taking place in our own rooms. Since we followed the same basic plan every year there wasn't much to discuss. We had the ability to watch each other and make small adjustments as needed as we went through each day.
- We did have lunch together on Fridays to enjoy being together and to talk about anything that was necessary. Betty said her husband would ask her on occasion during the week if Sudie had mentioned something about this or that. "My goodness," Betty would say, "we don't have any time to talk while we are busy with the children."
- I do think our lack of "staff meetings" was fine for the two of us, but not a good plan in general. It did not work so well when we later had more staff participating, morning and afternoon classes

using the same rooms, and more people who needed to be a part of the planning and management of everything.

- We did not do any formal group parent education. This was a similarity with the university lab schools in the '60s and early '70s. It was quite different, however, from the emphases of the Head Start work and the preschool co-op work I had done in the late '70s and early '80s. We did try to answer specific questions parents asked us from time to time if we could. Also, we had books about Montessori education and general books about early childhood that we could loan out to parents.

MANY MONTESSORI SCHOOLS ARE EXPENSIVE. WHAT WOULD YOU SUGGEST PARENTS CAN DO TO PROVIDE SOME OF THE SAME TYPE OF EXPERIENCES AT HOME?

- Remember, a Montessori education is about a lot more than activities. It is about respecting the child and helping to keep that inner flame burning. Value your child's interests and ideas and basic personhood. You can buy or make activities similar to Montessori ones to use at home, but activities need to be done in ways that help in the accomplishment of the big goals.

- Observe your child while he is working and playing. Do not interrupt your child when he is concentrating on something, especially before he has learned to concentrate well. Honor your child's interest and inner rhythms. Notice how your child solves problems.

- Spend a little time each day with each child individually with a good activity so that you can get to know the child better. I think ten minutes is a reasonable amount of time. Try to focus on that child and do not interrupt the session for other things unless absolutely necessary.

- Talk with your child. Read stories together. Sing songs. Count together. Encourage memorization of poems and retelling stories in your own words. Throw balls, run and climb, and swim. Study nature.

- Emphasize practical life activities. Teach your child how to zip, how to button, how to fold a napkin, how to pour from a little pitcher. Use slow motions and let the child practice after your demonstration. Do not expect perfection. Let your child help set

Montessori Work

the table, make the bed, and sweep the floor. Point out to the child the main idea of what you are trying to do. Give encouragement without overdoing the praise.

- Teach your children to put their clothes and activities away after using them. If each thing has a place, it is easier to locate it later. Piling toys in boxes may mean broken parts, things are hard to see and find, etc. (See the paper in Section II on Strategies I Observed in Montessori Schools that are adaptable in other situations. See Hancock's book for adapting Montessori activities for home use.)
- Teach your child good manners. Practice saying greetings and goodbyes and learning ways to say thank you. Teach your child to respect other people and to think about their needs.
- Try to provide situations where your child is building upon things he has already learned. Working puzzles that provide increasing difficulty is a good example of this.
- Playing games with your child like card games or checkers where he/she must learn the rules and the procedures for playing are helpful. (My mother liked to teach five- and six-year-olds to play Chinese checkers.)
- Teach your child the "three parts" to every activity: preparation, "doing," and clean-up.
- Keep a record with your children of what is going on in their lives. Pictures, write-ups, etc. can help document what the child is learning and doing. Let your child dictate some of his or her ideas to go with the photographs and pictures. Keep your journal record book handy for making additions and for the joy of looking at it and reviewing it.
- Help your child distinguish activities that are "follow the procedure" types from those that they should do "their way." Art activities seem to work especially well for the latter. Refer to the paper in Section II on Skills and Creativity. This is a particular interest of mine. I do not think that Montessori was aware of the full importance of creative art activities, but I do think we both believed in the dignity of the child and in trying to encourage the child's full development in many different areas.
- Simplify what you are teaching. Keep confusion at a minimum. Observe what might be standing in the way of your

child's progress. Support your child's learning and development consistently.

• Help your child to learn to behave appropriately in a variety of circumstances, etc. Help him/her learn to see similarities and differences in various situations. (See the article on Contrasts in Part II.)

• Trying to teach numbers and letters the Montessori way or any other way may be frustrating for parents since most parents are not trained in how to do this. As a parent, it is better to stick with educational activities that are successful for you and the child. There are many activities that parents can do with children to help lay a foundation for success in school other than explicitly teaching the written numbers and letters. (See all the things mentioned in the papers in Part II, as well as those mentioned in the answer to this question.)

MORE INFORMATION ON OUR PROGRAM

In reality, each part of the program had a direct or indirect impact on all other parts of the program and in daily practice aided and abetted each other.

THE TEN-MINUTE INDIVIDUAL LESSON

The individual lessons occurred as a part of activity time between nine and eleven-fifteen each day. At times children came and sat at the desk watching the lesson and eagerly awaiting their own lesson. If no one was waiting, the teacher would nod or smile at a nearby child who was not busy to come over for a lesson. In the first months of school, we did not call a child for a lesson while he or she was actively engaged and concentrating on an activity. One of our main goals was for the children to learn to concentrate on a chosen activity; therefore, we didn't want to interrupt them.

Even on the first day of school we gave an individual lesson to each child. This set the precedent that, for a short time during the two-hour activity period each day, each child had a little lesson. The initial period might be shorter than ten minutes. But the same procedure happened. The child came and sat by the teacher. The child paid attention to the lesson. The child responded with actions and words which reflected his or her understanding of the lesson.

No child was allowed to interrupt another child's lesson or answer the questions for that child. If a child not having the lesson needed to speak to the teacher, he or she could sit at her table and wait or stand quietly by. When the teacher came to a good stopping place she would attend to that child.

While at the lesson, the teacher was in charge and the child learned to begin and end the session at the teacher's discretion. I found from experience that if you allowed the children to take over the lesson and make the decisions about how long to work, what pages to read, etc., they might then want to argue about what, when, and how, the next day. Each teacher had only ten minutes or less for each child's lesson each day. Betty, I had noticed, seemed to stick to her one new page a day routine in the first set of books even though a child could often have read further. I think this paid off in the long run. It kept the progress to be made each day understandable to the child and the adult and not a matter of worry or contention.

The lesson was an important step for the child in focusing attention on something presented specifically to him/her. The lessons, like most M.M. activities were designed and presented in such a way that the children found them interesting. Also, the lesson was short enough that it ended on a positive note while the child was still paying attention and being successful.

We had many activities at the school that the child could begin and finish at his or her own discretion. It seemed quite valid to me that the child did learn to accept the teacher's authority as to the beginning, content, and ending of the lesson.

I was surprised at the overall impact of the daily, individual lessons on the teacher/child relationship in general. I believe it made it possible to know, understand, and enjoy the child in a special way. And maybe the children knew us better too from that "one on one" experience. I noticed that each child had a "modus operandi" that was much the same each day. It was easy to notice if the child's demeanor varied. Sometimes all it took was a minute to discover the problem, make a comment, have the child respond, and get on with the lesson. What the child shared often gave me new insights that would improve understanding of that child and maybe others too. Also, at group time because we knew many things that each child had mastered, we were able to include each child in a way that would be successful for him or her.

In the individual lesson, there was a momentum to the child's learning which was affected if many sessions were missed. This was especially true in the initial stages of learning numbers or learning letter sounds and reading.

Comments

I am aware that **most other Montessori schools do not present the individual lessons in this format—with ten minutes for each child each day.** I do believe that Betty's daily lesson might have been a special help for children with memory or attention problems. There would have been less time "to forget" the procedure, the expectation, and the knowledge base. It was also easier for the teachers to remember the nuances in the child's learning, and it was not necessary to keep many written notes because you could remember well from one day to the next. I liked Betty's method.

The individual lesson was not the only type of lesson we gave. Small group lessons and larger group lessons also were given from time to time, but not every day.

It could be that our preoccupation with the lessons also had a secondary advantage. We could not jump up and take care of every little thing that looked like a potential frustration or problem. The children knew this and often found ways to solve their difficulties.

I thought it was interesting that when I would ask older children that had come to our school what they remembered about our school, no one ever said it was the little lessons. I think the lessons were taken for granted like so many of the things that happen on a routine basis. Of course, that little lesson took only ten minutes out of the 135 minutes of the activity time for the child. For the teacher, about 120 minutes of that time was spent on individual lessons! I think I shall always remember those wonderful little lessons and those precious children sitting beside me.

SEGUIN'S "THREE STAGED LESSON"

One important technique used for teaching specific things

at the individual lesson time was "The Three Staged Lesson." Montessori (*The Discovery of the Child*, pp.156-158) credits Edward Seguin with the basic idea for this method of teaching. Today it is commonly spoken of as the **"Three Period Lesson."** M.M. used this technique to teach textures, colors, weights, numbers, letter sounds, etc. We found this to be a consistently effective teaching method. The following is a general description of a presentation to distinguish rough and smooth by feel and to learn the corresponding descriptive terms: rough and smooth. More specific information about this is found in the Montessori (*The Discovery of the Child*, pp. 156-158.) The following is the main ideas put into my own words.

Part I – Teacher shows and feels, and names; the child does the same: Adult feels surface of rough board and says, "Rough." Child does the same. Adult feels surface of smooth board and says, "Smooth." She moves and speaks slowly and deliberately. Child does the same. (Adult can softly say the rough or smooth word with the child as the child feels the texture in this part of the teaching.)

Part II - Teacher asks the child to point. (Being able to recognize an object by sight or feel and point to the object that the teacher has named or described is easier than looking at an object and remembering the word.) The teacher places both the rough and smooth boards on the table. She says to the child, "Point to the smooth." It is okay for the child to feel the texture to help him decide. If that is successful then she says, "Point to the rough." If the child does that successfully, the teacher proceeds to Part III.

Part III - Teacher checks to see if the child can associate the word with the object. The adult picks both objects up and puts them behind her back with the attitude of playing a little game. She brings out one board and looks at the child for a response of touching it and naming it. Then she brings out the other board for the child to touch and name.

SOME OF OUR EARLY INDIVIDUAL LESSONS

Smooth and Rough boards—General description of the lesson is given above. **Colors**—Use Montessori color tablets, set number two, either bought or handmade. **Shapes**—We used the wooden geometric shapes from the geometric cabinet. We began with two familiar yet contrasting shapes such as the circle and square for the first lesson on shapes. When demonstrating a shape, the teacher used the first two fingers of the dominant hand to follow slowly the outline of the shape while saying its name. We used the "Three Period Lesson" to teach the children to associate the correct name with each shape.

There is more involved in the lesson than just learning the specific concept being taught. The child is also learning to be comfortable **with the procedure** and with working with the teacher. The same or similar procedures will often be used as things get more complicated. That is why the initial lessons are always done slowly and carefully. In the first series of lessons it is often true that the child may already know one or both of the final answers, but that is okay. That may facilitate the ease of the early lessons.

TEACHING NUMBERS AND MATH CONCEPTS

Many sensorial exercises help the child build a foundation for understanding arithmetic. Among the Montessori activities we used for this were: The Pink Tower, Brown Stair, Long Rods, Knobbed Cylinders, etc. All these activities feature placing items in order from the largest to the smallest or vice versa. We generally introduced these to a small group of children rather than in individual lessons. We tried to be sure the children had these demonstrated to them, that they had practiced them, and understood these concepts before we began the arithmetic exercises.

We used the basic Montessori arithmetic exercises, The Number Rods, The Tactile Numbers, The Spindle Box, etc. (*The Discovery of the Child*, pp. 263-270) and we introduced them to the children either individually or in a small group at the appropriate time.

In our school, we presented the **tactile numbers** to each child during their individual lesson time. We began with 1 and 2. We used the Three Period Lesson to have the child copy the teacher in feeling and saying each number, secondly in pointing to the correct number the teacher had named and thirdly in being able to say the name when shown the number symbol by the teacher.

Concurrently we taught what quantities they represented by using little cubes for counting. The use of the little cubes was one of Betty's ideas.

The next day the numbers one and two were reviewed; if they are remembered then three was introduced. Sometimes the child was helped to remember the name of the number in Part III (of the Three Period Lesson) by feeling the tactile symbol. This was motor memory at work! Each day the numbers learned would be reviewed to check the child's mastery of them before a new number was introduced.

Other activities for number work

We had other things that aided and abetted our number work. Betty had found interesting activities with numbers. And when a child had mastered one through four, she would show that child the "four activity" which now they could take off the shelf to use anytime they desired. There were special games or activities for many of the numbers from four to ten.

During our snack time we used numbers by counting out the crackers or how many children were at each table. In group time we used finger plays that featured numbers and we sometimes played games that used numbers.

WRITING NUMBERS 1,2,3,4,5,6,7,8,9,10
BETTY'S METHOD

We taught the children to write numbers soon after they knew them from lessons with the tactile number cards. First we used the blackboard where a number can be made very big. The teacher wrote on the board with her finger and that left a faint roadway for the child to follow with the chalk. The teacher had emphasized where to begin by marking a small chalk dot on the blackboard. She emphasized where to end by stopping abruptly and lifting her finger away from the black board with emphasis. The child followed the faint roadway with the chalk and afterwards it was the child's number that was seen and not the teacher's finger mark. The child then practiced without the roadway on the blackboard. He copied the first number he made. After being able to do this, and making a few numbers without the "roadway," the child was ready to write on paper. Writing numbers was facilitated by having previously learned the numbers by feel as well as visually. The child had some motor memory of how each number symbol was formed before trying to write them.

We used a sheet of paper that had squares, ten in a row, and ten rows. For the first paper number work, only one or two rows were used; the big sheet was cut to appropriate size for each child. The teacher would make a mark showing where each number begins. In the beginning I often used my wooden pointer to make the form of the number in the square. It makes only the slightest indentation, with no color, but this gives the child a minimum guide as the roadway did on the blackboard. The child can then take the pencil and follow the faint indentation.

Some materials use dots or dashes to outline the numbers, allowing the child to trace over these marks to create the desired number. We did not use this method. I learned from Betty that in that system often a child goes from one dot or dash to the next and does not get the feel for the sweep and form of the number which he/she needs to remember and use consistently.

One little activity I frequently added to the beginning number writing was to ask the child to look over the numbers he/she had written on each row, and then choose the best number in each row and put a circle around it. They liked doing that and were always quite pleased with their judgments, and I was too.

ADVANCED NUMBER WORK

This work was introduced and practiced by a child or by several children together as they became ready for it. Often children did the work in pairs rather than individually. Usually these materials were being introduced to small groups of older children all through the year. Remember, the teacher had about ten extra minutes at the activity time when she wasn't engaged in individual lessons. Also, if a child were absent, the teacher would have a little extra time in which to give these "small group" lessons. Some number work was done at the group times.

Advanced number work included the use of Montessori's golden beads, the Seguin Board, learning to add and subtract, unison group counting to one hundred, writing to one hundred,

Montessori Work

putting number tiles in the right places on the "100" board, and writing numbers in a long list on paper from adding machine rolls. We also had a large frame with one hundred beads which were approximately one inch in diameter. These beads were on wires with ten in each row, five beads painted one color and five beads another color. This was one of Betty's great finds from a garage sale! At group time we could push the beads over one by one as the children counted to one hundred; we could push two beads over at a time and count by twos; five beads at a time to count by fives; ten beads at a time to count by tens. Also, the children could think of a number between one and a hundred and someone could come up and make that number with the beads!

Oh, yes, and there was another much enjoyed activity by the five-year-olds who were learning to add. It was called the Tens Game and it was played by two children with a deck of cards without the face cards. The ace was a one. The object of this game was to find pairs of cards that together would make ten. I'm not sure where Betty found this game! I also think she took out the face cards, put zeros on the jokers and only left two 10 cards in the deck...(to pair with the jokers). She had the children each receive four cards to begin with and the rest were in a pile in the middle. The children took turns picking up a card from the pile and seeing if it added with some number in their hand to make 10. Paired numbers were put aside. If no pair was made, the child discarded a card to the bottom of the pile.

Teen Numbers

If you pronounce the teen numbers as they are said in English, it is confusing for some young children to write them because we say the unit number first. For example with thirteen, the child hears "three" (thir), first and then "ten" (teen), but we write the ten first and then the three for the units. When the child began to write the teen numbers we often said one group of ten and 1 for eleven, 1 group of ten and 2, twelve, 1 group of ten and 3, thirteen...if the teacher said the one group of ten and __ while the child was writing the number there was less confusion in which number should be written first. There were many Montessori activities such as the Seguin Board and the Golden Beads that helped the children understand what the numbers meant.

In most of the classroom counting activities, the numbers were said in their regular English way. Frequently Betty's class at group time counted to one hundred in unison. Sometimes my class of younger children enjoyed doing it toward the end of a school year.

Writing to "100"

Our children loved doing this activity. After they had learned to write to "20" then it was easy to write to "30" and then soon further and further. As mentioned earlier, some children wrote far beyond one hundred. Sometimes to reinforce the understanding of the numbers I would ask a child to point to a certain number they had written on a paper. Find the "8," point to the "20," etc., or I might change it and say find the number that represents four groups of ten and five units. Sometimes Betty would let her children come to the blackboard at group time and write a number for the other children to recognize and name.

After retirement when I tutored elementary age children who had problems in arithmetic at school, I found they did not have the same fascination for writing numbers that our four- and five-year-old children had. I don't know if it was because they had picked up a dislike for numbers or whether they were past the point developmentally for this sort of repetition. Maybe it was some of both. Could it be that the Montessori children were not just repeating, but rather they were trying to improve the form and the speed with which they wrote those numbers and they were noticing relationships between the numbers in the various rows? Maybe this was similar to the practice of a great pianist!

OUR READING PROGRAM SEQUENCE

This program was based on phonics. It usually took a child two to three years to complete the whole program and become a fluent reader. Most of these activities were presented to the child during an individual lesson. One exception is the "I Spy Basket" used with a group. Other Montessori schools use some of the same materials that we did, but there was, and probably still is, great variation among schools in the actual teaching and practice of reading. It was a major subject at our school.

I Spy Basket to introduce listening for the first sound of a word. The basket contents are covered but the teacher lets a tiny portion of one object show and says: "I spy with my little eye, something that starts with, e.g., aaa." In that instance the "a" is a short "a" as pronounced in apple. (I had a lovely red wooden apple!) When the children spy a bit of the apple peeking out, they all say, "apple"... "aaa" for apple. I tried to find interesting and artistic items for the basket like a carved wooden zebra from Kenya, a tiny chartreuse cardboard box, a plastic octopus which made a squeak when you pinched him. We learned this activity from another Montessori teacher.

Montessori Tactile Letters – The teacher introduced these to the child at the Individual Lesson. It usually took from about two months or a little less for a four-year-old child to learn the short vowel sounds and the major sound for each consonant. Five-year-olds might do it in about six weeks.

Montessori Moveable Alphabet – The teacher demonstrated the use of this activity after the child knew most of the letter sounds. In a large flat box were found all the letters in separate little compartments. The activity also included miniature objects, e.g., cat, dog, pig, hat, rat, which were all in a small box.

Other Montessori Phonetic Material – Pictures of items that are three-letter phonetic words like cat, rat, leg, etc. pasted on tag board with corresponding words on tag board.

The "The Book" introduced the non-phonetic word "the" for the child to remember by sight. **The "A Book"** introduced the non-phonetic word "a" for the child to remember by sight.

Short Vowel Books: The first book series began with *Max* by Janis Raabe (Phonics Practice Readers, Series A, set 1, Modern Curriculum Press). There were ten books in all the series. The next two series were Primary Phonics books by Barbara Makar (Educators Publishing Service, Inc.) Set 1 began with *Mac and Tab* and Set M1 began with *The Cab*.

Introduction to Long vowels – Betty's adaptation of the story of the mother, children, guest, etc. adapted from *Reading with Phonics, Teacher's Ed.* by Hay and Wingo, pp.131, 132.

Montessori Long Vowel Material: Child practices words with long vowel sounds.

Special Books using long vowels and new phonetic rules were used as follows: Series beginning with *Kate and Jake,* Phonics Practice Readers by Janis Raabe, (Series A, Set 2, Long Vowels, Modern Curriculum Press). The next books were Primary Phonics Books by Barbara Makar (Educators Publishing Service). They were as follows: Primary Phonics set 2, beginning with *Mac is Safe;* Primary Phonics set M2, beginning with *Babe the Big Hit.*

Primary Phonics sets 3, 4, and 5 (Educators Publishing Service, Inc.) introduced the child to more complexities in Phonics.

Choose books to read from our little library.

LEARNING THE LETTER SOUNDS AND READING

We did not teach the names of the letters at this time in order to simplify what the child was dealing with. However, if a child knew the names, we would say that is good and now we will learn the sounds they make…because the sounds are a little different from the names.

We used the **"Three Period Lesson"** to teach the child two dissimilar letter sounds such as "a" and "s" with the tactile letter cards. The next day we reviewed the sounds learned by simply having the child follow the letter with his fingers and say the sound that it makes. If that was successful, we introduced a new letter. All the letters that have been learned before were reviewed each day before moving on to a new letter sound. If a five-year-old child learned one new letter a day, it took about six weeks to master all the letter sounds as mentioned earlier. If the child missed many days of school, it would take much longer because the success of the teaching/learning process was based on continual daily repetition. When the child returned to school, if he did not remember some sounds learned before, the teacher backed up and taught them again.

In teaching letter sounds to young children we found it best to use only **ONE** item consistently as the example of the sound. When we would introduce the tactile letter card and say the sound the first time we would also say the one word we planned to use with that sound such as: a (short sound) – apple, b – bat. The item is said immediately following the sound. This way the child clearly hears the sound and then the initial sound of the object is emphasized as it is said by the teacher. In reviewing at another time, if the child does not remember the sound that goes with a letter by looking at it, usually he will remember if he goes over the tactile letter with his finger. This is another example of the motor memory at work. Sometimes by feeling the letter the child may think of the object first and then recall the sound! We tried to think of objects that had something about them that was connected to the way a letter was made, e.g., for "m"…mountain, "s"…snake, "t"…tree, "z"…zigzag, etc.

Betty introduced the vowels first and emphasized them greatly. She also gave the children something to eat or taste or a little object that started with the short vowel sound, e.g., apple for "a," olive for "o," egg for "e," etc.

After the twenty-six sounds have been learned, the teacher demonstrates the moveable alphabet to the child. After the child does it successfully with the teacher, he/she can do it alone or with a friend.

Sometimes I played a game with letter sounds at group time. I'd say a word very slowly, emphasizing individual sounds, and the children listened and voiced the sounds, moving them closer and closer together until they could hear and recognize the word. I did not use the letter symbols. It was a listening game.

At the individual lesson time, after the child had learned all the sounds and successfully used the moveable alphabet and phonetic material, which I described earlier, the child was introduced to the sight word "the" with a little book that had "the" on each page. The child was first shown the word "the" written on a card. The teacher explained how to say it. Then she used the book and told the child to say "the" every time she pointed to it with her pointer. The child said "the" and the teacher said the other words on the pages. The next day the child reviewed "the" and used the special book for learning the sight word "a" (spoken similar to the short sound for "u"). The child said each word "a" and the teacher said the other words on the page. Sometimes I facilitated the child's remembering the correct sound by covering up the top half of the "a" with my pointer so that it looked like a "u."

I learned from Betty the use of **little wooden pointers**. They were like pencils with no lead. We made them from dowel material and then sharpened them in a pencil sharpener. We could point to the next word for the children and help keep their attention there. If necessary we could back up with the pointer and a child would try a word again. **This meant that we only needed actions with our pointer and we did not break the child's reading out loud with our own words**. I found that after the child had learned to read I could use the movement of the pointer to help him/her read along faster and to begin to put phrases together. The little pointer is an example of a little invention that was a big help.

After the child has learned the sight words "the" and "a," the next lesson was the introduction of the first book, *Max*. The words used in the first three books of the series were written on cards which were about two-by-eight inches. At the individual lesson, the teacher presented the cards to the child one at a time and the child sounded out each word. Then the child read one page in the book. The next day he sounded out, or said the words on the cards again, and then he read the first and second page. This continued in this fashion each day reviewing the words, reading from the beginning of the book, and adding one new page each day until the book was completed. The child then took the book home to read to his parents and was expected to bring the book back to school promptly. Other children would need the book.

Words for the remaining books in the first series were written on small pieces of paper and kept folded up in little boxes. The words for each book had a box of a different color. The child had the fun of opening up each little piece of paper and reading the words with the teacher before reading in the book.

At the end of the books in the Max series (and all the other books that we used from the Modern Curriculum Press) there were three statements from the book that the child had to put in order as to which happened first, second, or third. If we had played sequence games in class before these books were read, then the children usually understood the idea. Some of our young children needed extra help. The statements at the end of the book also provided a chance for the child to read a few sentences not in "context." This was a new learning experience. This activity also provided a chance for the teacher and child to review what had happened in the story and to let the child tell the teacher about it in his or her own words. It was a check on the child's comprehension of what had been read.

If a child at any point was not able to remember the work from the day before and do the new work today with relative ease, we found ways to back up. We would add supplementary material or extra books that would practice the known and proceed at a pace at which the child could succeed. I wrote some little books that could be used for these purposes as well as utilizing corollary sets at the school. But I was always glad when I could get back to the regular sets; the children seemed to track better and make more recognizable progress.

I noticed in the set beginning with *Max* that the books varied in difficulty. The first two were easier, the third was harder, the fourth was not so hard, and the fifth was very easy. I tried rearranging them one year and it was not so successful. Evidently the people who wrote the series had in mind something similar to sports training where we start easy, go for the more difficult, and then have something easy that makes the person feel like…wow, I can do this! Anyway, their way worked better!

At the beginning of a new year, we always had a returning child review numbers and letters and reread books from the year before in sequential order, usually one a day, and by November the child would usually be ready to get into new materials.

Betty had made a cardboard fold-up chart that showed all the basic sounds after the original consonant sounds and short vowel sounds. Often when a child was having trouble remembering a sound, if we took the chart and pointed to the sound, the child would remember it without our having to say a word. At times we supplemented our reading activities with materials in *Reading with Phonics* by Hay, Wingo, Hletko.

Learning Long Vowels
(Note: I designate the long vowel sounds in the section below with using the letter in bold format for the purposes of this explanation.)

Long vowels were introduced with Betty's adaptation of the little story from *Reading with Phonics, Teacher's Edition* by Hay and Wingo, pp. 131, 132. In the story a mother calls her children by their long names when company comes…so that instead of saying the child's nickname she would call him by his full name. That is a clue for the child that company has arrived and their behavior should change. There is an association made between the arrival of company and a change in the sounds to be made. The "e" at the end of the new words to be introduced is now referred to as the company and the child learns to use the "long name" of the preceding vowel and that the "e" at the end of these words is quiet.

Betty's extensive Montessori long vowel materials were beautifully handmade following the suggestions of St. Nicholas. After the introduction and practice with that material for the long letter **a,** the child was ready to read several pages in the book *Kate and Jake* (Phonics Practice Readers from Modern Curriculum Press). The following day, some of the information about the long **a** sound was reviewed and the child read maybe half of the book of *Kate and Jake.* On the next day the child read *Kate and Jake* from beginning to end and put the sentences in order at the back of the book. They then took that book home to read to the parents. The second book in the series also emphasized the long **a.** It could probably be read in two days.

The third book in the long vowel series featured the long **i** sound. Before reading the book, the teacher introduced the sound to the child with materials for learning the long **i** sound. The same format was followed as for learning long **a.** Then the child began to read in the appropriate book, *Bike Hike.* Learning the other long vowel sounds continues in the same fashion. The child finished all 10 books in that series.

For further practice with long vowels, the child read Primary Phonics series, sets M2 and 2, a total of 20 more books. He/she could usually read one a day at this point.

Advanced Phonics Books

Books in sets 3 through 5 in the Primary Phonics series (30 books) followed the introduction to long vowel books. The teacher pointed out to the child what particular new phonetic information was to be emphasized and showed the child where this particular information was located on her big chart. Usually the children were able to read a book a day.

Comments and Thoughts

I have tried to explain the methods we used in order to give the reader a feeling for how it came about that our children became good readers. Of course, not all children needed such explicit individual teaching, but some did, and with this method most children learned well if they were with us for at least a year before kindergarten and the kindergarten year too. The materials and the use of them were predicated on the teacher's awareness of each child and what he or she was ready for. It was always amazing to me how the pace changed from very slow and deliberate in the beginning to a little faster, and then for many children it was like the child was skating along with ease as the mastery grew. I think the most important part was the initial early foundation with the short vowels and major consonant sounds. That needed to be well mastered before beginning the long vowels in order for that part to move smoothly and fairly rapidly.

Another important element of our reading program was taking each book home to read to the parents. The child had immediate practice reading what he had already successfully completed at school, but now reading in a different setting to someone else. The parents took time to listen to the child. I am sure the parental support and interest greatly influenced the child's progress. Taking care of the books and getting them back to school in a timely manner was practice in "being responsible." Again each part of the program worked to complement and to support other areas of learning.

INSET DESIGN WORK
(Montessori, The Discovery of the Child, pp. 208-209)

This work was introduced to children who had already developed some eye-hand coordination by practicing the practical life and sensorial activities. Most of these children also had learned the concept of **start** and **stop**. They had learned to feel the major shapes and to know their names. They had probably been introduced to holding a pencil correctly and using it to write a few numbers before beginning this activity. Usually it was the four- and five-year-old children who were "ready" for this activity.

The Inset Design set we had was metal. There were five shapes with straight sides: square, triangle, rectangle, pentagon, and trapezoid. There were five shapes with curves: circle, oval, ellipse, curvilinear triangle, and a quatrefoil. Each shape had two forms: first as an inset frame with the shape (circle, square, triangle, etc.)

cut out of the middle of a square piece of metal, and secondly there was a corresponding metal shape to fit in every inset (circle, square, triangle, etc.) The latter pieces had little knobs.

This activity helped the child develop greater eye-hand coordination, pencil control, and joy in shape and color. It was an activity which became successively more and more complex and interesting as the initial skills were mastered.

We usually gave a small group demonstration on how to do this to children that we thought were ready to learn this. We used good colored pencils which would leave strong, definite marks. Before the first demonstration for the new children, they probably had watched returning children work on these designs. They may have noticed a few designs on the bulletin board. We displayed beginning and intermediary designs as well as those that were very complex and fully colored.

The children were encouraged to try a design after they had seen a demonstration. The main idea in the beginning was to follow the procedure and to get the design squared with the paper. This was important because soon the children would be placing a second inset shape on top of the first one. The shapes would line up pleasingly if they had been properly centered. The next important things were to draw lines that were mostly parallel and starting and stopping on the perimeter of the shape.

One time I had several children who did not stop when they came to the other side of the shape. To help them understand this concept, I played a game with my twelve children at group time. I made a big shape, such as a rectangle, with yarn. I demonstrated by standing on the yarn, saying, "start," and walking across the rectangle. When I got to the other side I stopped abruptly and said "stop." Each child got a turn. They enjoyed it! Without further explanation, I noticed they all made an effort to stop when they got to the line that marked the other side of the shapes in their next designs.

We did not really interfere with the children while they were working. We let them complete the design as best that they could with the information they had gathered from the initial demonstrations. Of course, it would have been very difficult for us to give our little individual lessons if we had to jump up all the time. All in all, it worked for everyone's benefit.

Montessori Work

Most of our children tried to follow the instructions for this activity. This was due in part to the fact that it was not introduced to a child until we had observed from other work that the child was doing that he would most likely be ready for this and find it interesting. I would be careful to explain to the child that this was a "follow-the-instruction" type of activity in the beginning, but there were a few things that the child could choose, such as which shape and which color of pencils.

I made a limit of two sheets of the special-cut inset design paper each day for each child. This encouraged the children to focus on the shape they had made and to color at least some part of it with the colored pencils. Sometimes a child would put a shape in his or her locker and go back an hour later and take it up to work on it some more.

For many children in their kindergarten year with us, making "inset designs" became a very skilled and much beloved activity. The children sat with their friends talking quietly while they worked. They often showed interest in each others' shapes and color combinations. No two were ever alike! I did notice that each child developed some uniqueness in the way he or she colored with the pencils. Some children made dark lines and bright bold colors. Some preferred lighter lines with less pressure. Some went back and forth, and some went only one way with the lines. I could usually recognize who had made a design without seeing any name.

The children figured out how to make stars by using the triangle inset and then inverting it. They also made great Easter egg designs with the oval shape. It was an endlessly fascinating activity. It was similar to a craft activity in that the child followed the instructions, but also there was opportunity for the child's unique ideas and skills to be apparent.

As with many Montessori activities, there were multiple "learnings" for the children. One I have not emphasized was the development of good control of the pencil. We taught the children the conventional, proper way of holding a pencil. In later teaching years I called it the **Power Pinch.** The kids loved that name. I had a triangular plastic piece they could be put over the pencil to help them remember to use the proper grip if it was difficult. Later when the children began to write words, this practice with the pencil was most helpful as they did not have to concentrate on how to hold the pencil or how to make it do what they wanted it to do. They only had to think about writing the words.

MUSIC ACTIVITIES AT OUR SCHOOL

On Fridays, when we sang songs as a group, we emphasized songs that children might sing with their families. We wanted to use songs that the parents might have learned when they were children. Many of these had hand actions to accompany the songs, e.g., "Twinkle, Twinkle, Little Star," "The Itsy Bitsy Spider," "The Wheels on the Bus Go Round and Round," "If You Are Happy and You Know it Clap Your Hands," etc. Other favorite songs were: "Mary Had a Little Lamb" (all the verses), "ABC Song," "The Continent Song," "Old MacDonald had a Farm," and "Bingo."

We also played little traditional singing games like, "Hokey Pokey," "Farmer in the Dell," "London Bridge," etc. We practiced moving to different rhythms and foot movements with a record that had selected music for skip, tiptoe, run, walk, etc. At rest, we sometimes listened to quiet classical music. Sometimes parents came and led the singing. Occasionally we had a parent or visitor come and play an instrument such as the harp, the clarinet, and the trombone.

Several different years we made puppets and performed "Peter and the Wolf." First we read the story and listened to the music. The children liked making different motions for each instrument as it was played. The children enjoyed having the parents come and watch the puppet show. One year we had to repeat it three or four times so that every child got a chance to use the puppet of one of his or her favorite characters.

TRACING BOX OR LIGHT BOX

I don't remember how we came up with the idea for this. It might have been from a catalogue or something I had seen in another school. It was similar to the lighted box used for viewing negatives or photographic slides that I had seen in a print shop. My husband made this light box for our school. It sat on a small table. It had a dimmer switch to turn the light on and off and for varying the intensity of the light source. It was about thirteen by nineteen inches by six inches or so deep. The surface above the light was a piece of hard, thick, semi-translucent plastic.

I wanted this originally in order to have a good way for children to use the outlines that had come with our science puzzles. Each puzzle had arrived with a simple outline on heavy stock, white paper. One set of puzzles included five different dinosaurs and the other set included five different animals, each animal representing a major category in the animal kingdom (elephant for mammals, a frog for amphibians, a duck for a type of bird, etc.). I had been in a quandary as to how to best use the outlines since I was not interested in photocopied material for the children. I decided that a "light box" for this activity might work.

The children put the paper with the outline of the object to be traced on the plastic surface. They put a clean piece of paper on top of the paper with the object. They had to hold these together with one hand while they followed the outline with a crayon. If the child had trouble holding the paper still, he/she could tape the papers down with removable tape.

I had great reservations about the "Tracing Machine" initially. I was afraid that it would hamper the children's creativity. However, I was careful about the objects for the tracing machine and about how I presented it to the children. I did not use any people or houses or pets or things that I thought the child might have an emotional connection to; I wanted these subjects to remain free for the child's own interpretation.

This was more like a craft activity. The children followed the instructions for making the outline, then they could use watercolors and paint their picture or they could use markers, crayons, or a combination of all three. I noticed that most children added decoration to their picture.

Usually it was the four- and five-year-olds who were interested in using this activity. However, they also continued to paint at the easel and to draw with the crayons in very creative ways. **They did not substitute this for their own start-to-finish paintings and pictures.** To me this was vitally important.

One day an interesting thing happened. I allowed a child to color or paint an outline that had been made by some other child. She had found it lying around and asked me if she could use it. I observed that as the child painted and worked on the project, she was not showing much interest in it. She quickly painted over the outline shape without showing care in her work. In her own work she had always worked carefully. I did not comment to the child about this because I felt it was my poor judgment that caused the problem.

I decided that making one's own outline was a significant part of the project. Maybe if you have gone to all the trouble to pick out a picture, study it, trace the outlines deliberately you would already have invested a lot in your project. You would then naturally care about painting it in a special way that would be attractive and interesting to you.

Or maybe having made the outline shape you have some sort of motor memory (re: Montessori) that makes the shapes stand out in your mind more clearly than just by looking at them. After seeing what happened with this child, I always had a child make his or her own outline. Of course, this whole scenario made me just more certain of some things I had been thinking about for a long time regarding the importance of "owning" your work from start to finish.

CALENDAR PROJECT

This was one of the great projects that Betty had invented. I must have done this project with children over 140 different times...once a month for all the years at our school. It was never boring. The children were drawn to it and seemed to like especially the fact that they knew the procedure. It was like a group tradition. We tried to do it the first day of each month.

There were four **major** parts to the project: 1. the numbers, 2. the drawing, 3. gluing the number paper down onto the big paper, 4. putting stickers and stars on special places.

1. Numbers – We bought special manila paper that was pre-printed in one-inch squares. We cut the sheets of paper so that each sheet had seven squares across the top and was usually five squares vertically, sometimes six depending on how the days fell in any particular month. A small border was left around the entire seven-by-six-inch sheet. The purpose of the border was to allow the teacher to write the days of the week above each vertical row.

Also, the tiny space at the bottom allowed the children to see the line for the base of the numbers on that row.

Before the teacher gave the paper to the child to begin the numbers, she put a small "x" in each square where there should be **no number**. And she made a very light "1" in the square where the month began. Children who knew how to write numbers well could proceed from there and fill in all the blocks appropriately. Children who needed a little help would stay at the teacher's desk and work there until they finished, in case they needed help. The number paper was completed during the work/activity time.

When the children first entered our school, they usually could not write any numbers and they did not know much about calendars. In their individual lesson time on the first day of the month, I would tell them the name of the new month and point out on the little squared paper where it said, Sunday, Monday, Tuesday, Wednesday, Thursday, Friday, Saturday. They liked to say the days of the week with me. Next I would show them on which square the first day of the month would be, and I would begin to write the numbers and encourage the child to count along with me if they wished.

Usually by October or November most of the three-years-olds could make a "1" and maybe a "2" and "3"…so the child made the numbers he/she could make. Sometimes I would provide a little help so he could make a few more. The manila paper was soft and I could make the number with my wooden pointer bearing down just enough to slightly mark the paper and the child could follow the flow of that slight indentation and usually make a few more numbers if he wanted to. Each teacher knew exactly how many numbers the child knew and could write. This way the teacher kept the expectation in line with what the child could complete successfully. Usually an older child would be glad to finish the numbers for a little one or in some cases the teacher might write the rest of the numbers as she and the child counted together.

This plan was used month by month and the children would be able to write more numbers each succeeding month. Then the child would reach a point where he/she could write numbers well, but going from the first row to the second might be problematic. In our regular number writing work the child wrote to "10" in the first row of squares and the numbers in the next row of course repeated the unit digit from the square directly above. In the case of the calendar, this did not happen. To help with this, we wrote very lightly the first number for each row and that cued the children how to proceed.

2. Drawing – At the group time, (the final half-hour of the day), the teacher handed out to each child a large sheet of plain manila paper (twenty by twelve inches) that had been folded in half. The children were told to put the fold at the edge of the table next to their bodies. Each child was handed a box with eight crayons in it. These boxed large crayons were saved for very special activities like the calendar and the yearbook picture. The children were asked to draw a picture for the month of _____. They generally drew whatever they liked: a design, a house, a family, a monster, etc. After the pictures were completed, the children were instructed to turn the paper over so that the fold was now facing away from them.

3. Pasting – The number paper was to be placed in the center of the bottom part of the folded paper. The teacher gave a short demonstration of putting a dab of paste in each corner on the back of the number paper. There were small jars of paste on each table and the children took turns using the paste. After all the number papers were pasted down, it was time to put on the special stickers.

4. Stickers – The teacher had the stars and holiday stickers for the children to apply to their number paper. For the first calendar of a school year, the teacher would have the children point to the x's on their paper (in the squares where there were no numbers), one by one, and slowly count them with her. That was how many stars each child would need. Next she showed how to place the stars exactly on top of the x's. Each child was given the appropriate number of stars. They proceeded to cover the x's. The children, especially the very youngest, loved covering the x's! Sometimes I let the very youngest children count out the x's with me at their lesson time and that made it easier for them to follow when I showed the group.

We also had stickers to go on the date for each holiday. For instance, in November we had a U.S. flag sticker for Veteran's Day. The teacher would say something like, point to the "11" on your paper. And for the youngest ones she might add, "It looks like this"...as she made an "11" in the air or on the blackboard. Older children could help the younger ones. The teacher explained that November 11 was Veteran's Day. If time permitted she might add more about the holiday. Then she would hand out the stickers. For some holidays, there would be a choice of stickers. For instance, for Thanksgiving the child might choose a turkey, a picture of Pilgrims and Native Americans, or a picture of the Mayflower. The children always enjoyed the stickers.

To finish the project, the name of the month had to be written above the number paper. Older children might want to copy it off the blackboard. Four-year-olds might want the teacher to write it in pencil and then they would go over it in a color of their choice. The youngest children might want the teacher to write it for them on their paper. The child would put his name on his work or the teacher would write it if necessary. Crayons were returned to the boxes and collected for storage. The project was completed and now ready to be taken home with each child.

Comments – The calendar project was good for a multitude of reasons.
- It gave the children a chance to use the numbers they had learned in a slightly different way.
- It introduced the concepts of keeping track of time by months and days and also by years. For January we always emphasized the New Year and had a special sticker for January first. The children especially liked the sticker of the new baby with a ribbon for the New Year.
- It introduced the children to a lot of holidays that we might honor with a special project or celebration when the day arrived. So it helped the children to look forward to the month's activities.
- Also, if there was a day that was to be a "no school day," that day could be noted on the calendar to remind the children and parents. The teacher could add a note at the bottom of the calendar to further explain these special days.
- It was useful at home. It could be posted the whole month and the child and family could use it like any other calendar. Friends and relatives who visited in the home might notice it and make conversation with the child about it.

- The calendar project concerned something that children would continue to learn more and more about. It was not an isolated bit of information that would have little future connection with the child.
- I am sure that in the beginning most of the younger children did not understand very much about what it meant. I think that is okay. That was in **contrast** to the many activities in our Montessori school that were only introduced to each of the children as they were ready to understand them. Even some parts of this project were understandable to the young child, e.g., pasting, putting on the stars, and drawing a picture. And of course, as the child got older and learned more, he understood more.

Comments

I smile when I think back over the occasional times that a child had not put the fold of the paper toward his body…in that case the picture turned out to be on the bottom half of the large paper. So what to do…we solved it various ways. Sometimes we just cut the paper in half and taped it together so the picture would be at the top. Or if the child wanted, we just put the number paper on the top half, etc.! It was all part of the process of learning.

I do not know how this project would work in other classroom situations. **The success of most projects is dependant on the skills and knowledge that the children already have, and how the project is presented and managed by the teacher. The fact that the project itself can be done in a reasonable time frame and that neither the children nor the teachers feel stressed out over it is also important.**

CONTINENT BOXES AND OUR GEOGRAPHY WORK

This is a simple idea, but I do not remember hearing of it being done elsewhere. I bought plastic boxes which were about ten inches wide by eighteen inches long by six inches deep and used one for items from or about each continent. The top of each box was decorated with a small cut-out facsimile of the particular continent (a map) that was featured in this box. The cut-out was made by tracing around the continent piece from the Montessori world puzzle and it was the same color as the puzzle piece of that continent. The children could immediately identify which continent box it was.

We added new items to the boxes as we found things for them. Of course, I had many things for the North America and South America box. Sometimes parents or grandparents brought back craft items from trips to other countries. My friend Judy Gazard brought me most of the items for the Australia box on one of her trips back to her home country.

Contents of Boxes:

North American Box:
- An orange felt mat to put on the floor for displaying the items
- Canadian Mountie wooden toy
- Pictures of animals from North America
- Money from Canada, U.S., and Mexico each in a separate container
- A *mola* (reverse appliqué fabric and needlework) from Panama
- A ceramic mug and saucer from Mexico
- A box of cards showing different Native American groups
- Books about North America
- Handmade "First Nations" doll from Canada

South American Box
- A pink felt mat
- A small toy llama
- Copper box from Chile
- A bracelet from Chile
- A matching game of the flags of all the South American countries
- Books about South America
- Woven hat from Peru
- Pictures of South American animals

European Box
- Several dolls from Europe

- A red felt mat
- Flag matching game
- Ribbons of different Scottish plaids and a book on the plaids
- A lotto game in Russian
- Russian set of dolls of different sizes that fit inside each other
- Little book in Danish for small children
- Small ceramic mug from Germany
- Wooden shoe from Holland
- *Peter and the Wolf, Little Red Riding Hood* story books

Asian Box
- Little set of wooden Japanese houses, one fitting in the other
- Replica of an Asian elephant made of ebony
- Book on China, book with Chinese writing
- Chopsticks
- Small intricately decorated box from India
- Japanese clogs for a small child
- Flag matching game of Asian countries
- Favorite story books about Asia or from Asia; e.g., *The Story About Ping, How My Parents Learned to Eat, A Pair of Red Clogs*

African Box
- Carved wooden mask from Kenya
- Shield made from animal skin from Kenya
- Flag matching game
- Books about different parts of Africa
- Beaded bracelet
- Family of African elephants made out of hard plastic
- *My Painted House, My Friendly Chicken, and Me* by Maya Angelou
- A book showing paper dolls from Africa and many different types of clothing
- A hand-carved zebra from Kenya

Australian Box
- A play boomerang decorated with Australian animals
- A koala
- A kangaroo
- A kookaburra puppet

Montessori Work

- An echidna
- Books about Australia
- Australian flag
- Pictures of animals like the platypus, black swan, etc.
- ABC book of Australian animals
- A tape of Australian music for children

Antarctica Box
- Some realistic penguins made out of hard plastic
- A story about Antarctica
- Big map of Antarctica

Each box also contained a small book that I had written and illustrated about the particular continent. It was fairly short and contained information I thought my young children would find interesting. I was sorry that these were not written until late in my teaching career. Most of the children I had taught never saw them.

The continent boxes were introduced one at a time in the classroom. At the beginning of the year the North American box was introduced to the children. They were shown the proper way to handle the objects and how to pack the box up with the biggest and flattest items put in the bottom of the box first. The children learned to look at the items carefully and place them on the mat in a way that they liked. None of the dolls, animals, or other items were to be used for play. They were to look at and handle carefully. The box was on a shelf and was one of the activities the children could choose during work time. Usually by November or December, the South American box as well had been introduced and was available to the children also.

I sometimes introduced Australia in January because I liked to play-out having a summertime picnic by pretending we were in Australia where it was summer. We would set up our Australian animals around the room and pretend they were watching us from their homes in the bush. The children loved it! In February, I might introduce the Asia box; and in March, maybe Europe; and in April, Africa; and last of all in May, Antarctica.

We had in our school the Montessori puzzle maps: the World, North America, South America, Africa, Europe, and Asia. We did not have a puzzle map for Antarctica. We did have a United States puzzle map. I tried to color code things. The mat for each box was the same color as that of the continent as painted on the Montessori world puzzle.

We frequently sang the continent song to help the children remember the names of the continents. Sometimes children brought items for show and tell that were made on other continents. Occasionally, we had visitors in the room from some other continent also.

We continued our work on the continents throughout the whole year. Sometimes we used Mexican songs and customs for our Christmas program. At Easter time I would read *Rechenka's Eggs* by Patricia Polacco and we would find Russia on the globe and on our puzzle maps. I tried to have several stories from each continent that we read when we were either studying that continent or celebrating a custom from that continent, such as Chinese New Year.

Sometimes I told stories in Spanish with only a few English words and lots of body language and hand expressions to help the children understand. They loved it!

BIRTHDAY CELEBRATIONS

Birthday celebrations at our school were done a number of different ways during my fifteen years there, but I will relate the one that worked the best for me. We had traditions about the way we celebrated. Children knew that when their birthday came, they would have a chance to choose different things, like the friend to hold the candle, playing color-shaped bingo, or reading birthday books. I am not sure who had thought up all the ideas that we used.

Parents were asked if they wished to bring a special treat for the birthday—candles on a cake were not an option, however. Usually the parents came to the party and brought special snacks and helped with the clean-up. Sometimes they planned special activities for the party. This took the place of the regular group activity for that day.

After the snack the children gathered in a semicircle and the birthday child chose a friend to hold a large, yellow, spherical candle that stood for the sun. The birthday child held a small globe showing the oceans in blue and the continents in tan. The candle for the sun was lit. The birthday child with globe in hand would begin walking slowly around the sun (at a safe distance) as many times as he or she was old. I would become narrator, describing for the rest of the class Johnny's travels with the earth around the sun. "Johnny was born on Oct. 10. It was in the fall. After fall, (and the child has walked one-quarter of the way around), winter came, then spring, then summer, and when fall came again, Johnny was one year old." (Johnny has now completed one circle.) "Then after fall, winter, spring, summer, and fall came again Johnny was two years old." (Johnny has now completed two circles.) The children say the years with me and also the seasons...now, winter, spring, summer, fall. Johnny was three years old. When we came to the age he was celebrating, I said something to the effect that, "now he is four!" (or whatever age). Then we sang "Happy Birthday." We always included a second verse which was "Many more of them too, many more of them too, many more happy birthdays, happy birthday to you!"

The birthday child was given a choice of playing color/shape bingo or of having a birthday story read. Most children chose the bingo game. We usually had time to play three games. The prizes were plastic beads. (Betty had a friend who sent her a box of beads left over from Mardi Gras each year.) The winners came up first to choose their beads and then each child got a chance to choose beads for being "a good player."

The game helped teach the children to pay attention, follow instructions, learn patience, learn the names of shapes and colors, and deal with the excitement of a party. In the years that I had the younger children I would play the game for fun with no prizes early in the year before any birthdays. I would also prearrange the cards used so that practically everyone would get to cover up something about every other time. That way the children understood what was happening and it didn't take too long to complete a game.

When we played the game for a birthday party we often had a younger child sit next to an older child, or else we would request the parents help the younger children as needed. This game was different from most of our activities in that it did involve some chance. Once we had a child very upset because he said at this school everything was supposed to be about how hard you tried. He complained that he had tried hard, paid good attention, and did not win. This was his first game of chance and it was a new concept. (This child might have benefited from more preparation or maybe he was voicing what many young children might initially feel in that situation. In my early training in the late 1950s we were advised not to play any game with three- and four-year-olds where there was "a winner." This was a concept they were not ready for (according to the teaching of that day.) At our school, most of the children seemed to enjoy this game; they looked forward to choosing their beads, and they were not too upset about "not being the winner." The use of games of chance would be a good topic for parents and preschool teachers to think about and discuss. I do not remember that I played any games with "winners" in the other preschool settings I had worked in, but I do remember playing such games in my own childhood. I never won very frequently. This would be another interesting topic for parents and teachers to discuss. Do games of chance have value? When? Where? Why?

I thought in our class that maybe this was an important contrast to our regular activities. We tried to include things at holiday time, birthdays, and sometimes in general group that where definitely a **contrast** to activities that were a part of our major work time.

Interestingly enough, we had lots of books about birthdays but one book was by far our favorite. It was about hard luck (although the author did not call it that), and persistence and love that brought about a happy ending. It was the story of a dad who had ten miles to go to get home for his child's birthday. He started in his car, but after one mile, it broke down. After each mile there was some problem and he had to change to another method of transportation. Finally he arrives home walking and barefooted, but package in hand. At the end of the book, the package could be opened and there were pictures of many different little toys. We let the birthday child tell what she/he would have chosen from that box. Our children never seemed to tire of this book from year to year. (We no longer have this book and I have not been able to locate its author or title.)

Montessori Work

HANDMADE MATERIALS by Bill and Sudie
- Wooden shelves
- Tactile numbers
- Tactile letters
- Moveable alphabets
- Long rods
- Two trays with eight bells in each for matching tones
- Tracing machine
- Four little wooden tables for children doing individual work
- Felt covers for the large set of bells
- Boxes for matching bells
- A board with little doors that had various latches and locks
- Color mixing activity
- Walking board
- Land and water forms
- Shelf for the geography puzzles
- Matching game for different kinds of wood from trees common in our area
- Practical Life activity which featured boxes with a variety of tops
- A board with bolts from small to large with a nut to fit each bolt
- Matching-type game with different little shells glued to each side of wooden pieces, about domino size
- Stacking circle game made of wood – all same color and thickness…variation in diameter of circle only. Circle discs were stacked on a fixed post attached to a circular base.
- Several sets of science cabinets: tiny drawers with matching cards for birds, reptiles, mammals, trees, plants, flowers, etc.
- Books about each continent – written and illustrated by Sudie
- Short little books for early reading with words the children could sound out. These books were about things that the children knew about and they were meant to be interesting, not silly. I had also drawn my own little illustrations which the children liked.
- A board cut with long wavy grooves for the purpose of practicing use of the first two fingers together to follow an irregular "path." This little invention was very useful and children were fascinated by it. This gave the children a way of practicing,

i.e., holding the two fingers together. That method would be used with feeling around the perimeter of shapes and feeling the formation of the numbers and letters with the tactile materials.

A FEW CRAFTS OUR CHILDREN ESPECIALLY LIKED

The Tape Picture Craft is a good activity for early in the year. It can be done with children of many ages. Children are given a short demonstration in how to cut pieces of colored tape from the roll. Each child is then given half of a piece of dark construction paper (black works well...brightly colored tape shows up better here than on colored or white paper). Then the children proceed to make their pictures from the little pieces of tape they cut. The younger children just enjoy cutting, putting the tape down randomly or piling it on top of itself. The older children often make houses or stick figures with the tape.

Leaf Rubbings Craft - To do this successfully with young children the leaves need to be secured to the table or board and then the child's paper needs to be taped on top so it will not slip. Give a demonstration showing the use of the side of the crayon and the type of stroke that makes the veins in the leaf stand out. I have found this project best done during work time, with only one or two children working at the table at a time. Some types of paper work better for this than others. Removable tape will work to hold the child's paper down. I have also found that having several layers of newspaper underneath everything will help. Using fairly small leaves also makes it easier. Often we do this project as the leaves begin to turn colors and we also have a leaf puzzle for classroom use. Children are encouraged to bring leaves from home for show-and-tell and to tell us about the tree they came from.

One year I tried putting some leaves vein side up on top of contact paper. Then the child put their paper on top and there was enough "adhesion" to hold everything in place for the rubbing. This worked nicely, especially after several children had used it. You have to be quite careful removing the first several pictures so that the child's paper does not tear coming off. After I noted this problem, I tried putting several pieces of blank paper down and removing it several times from the contact paper. This produced a surface that wasn't quite so sticky. Use your imagination and figure out what works best in your situation.

Torn Paper Ghosts pasted on black construction paper – a Halloween craft. Children can tear off pieces to make little ghosts from newsprint or some other type of paper. Almost any shape can look like a ghost! The children can draw big eyes on the ghosts. (Black markers make strong eyes.) Children can tell a story about their ghosts also.

ABC Halloween Book – This is a rather complicated project in which each child begins with a large sheet of paper and ends up with a little book. There are stickers for some pages and drawings for others. I will not try to explain how to do the project since it is very hard to make it understandable without a picture. I did learn something that I would like to share with you from this project. Sometimes I tried to do the activity with other children (nieces, nephews, great grandchildren, etc.) outside of my regular preschool class. In retrospect, I do not think it was as interesting to those children because they had not had a strong foundation for the project.

In class we had read and enjoyed a similar, but larger, ABC Halloween book at group time before we did the project. We went over this book many times in October before we began the project. Some children had done it in previous years. Therefore, those children in the preschool class had a good foundation for the project. I have noticed that at times there is a contagious joy with some group activities. Another contributing factor to success was that there was a certain time of day set aside for this project... whereas outside of class, the children probably had other things on their minds that they really wanted to do. I think the children outside my class were intrigued a little with the project because maybe they had never seen 1 big sheet of paper which was made into a little book and of course they liked the stickers!

Bracelets made from an envelope – Using a size-10 business envelope, seal the envelope. On the side for addressing the envelope draw thick lines approximately one inch apart vertically across the narrow dimension of the envelope. (It looks like a ladder.) Demonstrate to the children how to cut on the lines. Children cut on the lines and then have bracelets to decorate. This is a craft that was greatly enjoyed by all ages and is very easy to set up. The children used crayons or markers for the decoration and sometimes they used repeat designs or colored them solid colors. They liked to exchange them with each other or take them home to Mother as a gift.

Other craft activities were paper chains, the Christmas Yule log (discussed earlier), making valentines, cutting out a big green shamrock for St. Patrick's Day, dying Easter eggs, making an Easter bunny basket from a paper sack, making a pinch pot or a coiled pot from clay, weaving with paper strips, weaving pot holders on a little loom, and spatter painting dried flowers and weeds to make stationery for Mother's Day presents.

YEARBOOK PROJECT

Each year we made a yearbook for each child. The first pictures in the yearbook were the nine pictures drawn by the child, a different one each month. We used a little heavier and better quality paper for these pictures than what was put out for regular drawing paper. The teacher printed the topic at the bottom of the paper ahead of time. We asked the children to draw a picture with crayons to go with a certain idea. Below is the list of the topics for each month as they appeared most years.

- September: My name is _____.
- October: This is my house.
- November: This is my mother.
- December: This is my father.
- January: This is my _____ (sister, brother, cousin) or, These are my _____s.
- February: I like to play.
- March: I like to work.
- April: These are my friends.
- May: I am_____.

It was always interesting to see how the children's art work developed during the year. From month to month, I could often see the growing complexity and vitality in their drawings and paintings. Parents could see the changes easily, comparing the September picture the child had drawn of himself with the later one in May.

Montessori Work

We also included photographs of the children in the school in each child's book, usually two children in a picture, and these pictures were in everyone's book. Also, everyone had a class picture and a picture of the teachers. Extra pictures were also taken some years. These might be individual pictures, pictures doing special work, pictures from a field trip or holiday party.

Some of the child's work from the year was included in the book. Usually there would be three or four inset designs which had been colored with the colored pencils. Also there would be examples of number work. The young children might have written to "10." The four-and five-year-olds often completed writing papers to "100," and they would choose one that they thought especially well done to include in the yearbook. There might be a map of the world with the continents colored like they are on the Montessori puzzle map and on the Montessori globe. There might be some original drawings the child had made during the year with crayons, markers, or watercolors.

The children chose the color of construction paper they wanted for the front and back of the book. It took the teachers many hours getting the photographs together, collecting and keeping samples of each child's work, mounting everything in each book, but I always felt it was well worth the effort, and I am sure I was as proud of each child's book as he or she was! It was a great way to end the year.

Many parents have told me that they have saved their children's yearbooks and treasure them as a reminder of those years and the child's experiences in the school. This project that was completed at the end of each year at Montessori Community School makes a good place to close this section of my book.

Part VII
Bibliography

In Memory of **May Kluttz**

May was the first person other than my mother that I remember to introduce me to the wonderful world of children's books. She and my mother had been in college together. Later they were teachers in the same school and they roomed and boarded in the same home in Winston Salem, N.C. May became an art teacher after several years teaching other grades. In my childhood we received a special book from May "for Christmas" each year. These books usually arrived, however, in the summer! What surprise and joy they were. Sometimes the books were about the life of children in other countries, such as the d'Aulaires' *Ola*. I'm sure that they were very influential in my developing an interest in the whole world, and they certainly fostered my interest in art and in illustrations in children's books.

May was somebody to reckon with all her life. In Atlanta where she taught high school art classes for many years there was something called "May's Thunder." The story went like this:

Sudie Doughton Mason

When some organization in town wanted some great decorations for an event, they would call in Miss Kluttz. She, with the help of her students and whatever they could find and put together, always came up with surprising and outstanding decorations. May and her classes were the original creative "Recycle People!"

Years later, I would call May now and then just to talk. Once there was a terrible storm that had hit Concord, N.C., where she and her sister then lived. My mother, in a town one hundred miles away, could not get through to May, and she was worried about them. Mother called me and I called May. I got through somehow, and then got back to Mother with news of their situation. May, answering the phone in her normal cheerful voice, responded to my questions about their welfare with, "Yes, Sudie. We are just fine...thanks to our good neighbors!"

"And what did the neighbors do?" I queried.

"Oh, they brought the flashlight," she replied.

I have always remembered her remark and have thought that we never know the power of one flashlight. Books are kind of like flashlights. They can help us see. And they are especially valuable when the information is something you can use. And sometimes they even illuminate things we did not know were even out there!

Foreword

After searching all over the house and basement, I have lugged these books to my office and have them sitting around me in haphazard piles on the floor and on my desk. It has been an unexpected great pleasure to look at them again and hold them in my hands. And there is some significance to having them all close around me together rather than simply going to a shelf, picking one out, and looking at it all alone. As I reach for first one book and then another I notice that I change my "modus operandi" often. Sometimes I seek out the needed information for the bibliography entry first and then glance through the book. Other times I look at it a first and then get the information for the entry. Sometimes I reread at the beginning or the end. Sometimes I notice the things I underlined or I am reminded of the impact this author made on my thinking in a certain way. And I read the preface.

Before this exercise in "book writing" I never read a preface. I was so intent on getting into the subject matter. Now I am reading the prefaces and the forewords and the acknowledgements; they all send a wonderful sense of what the writer was all about. They are good things to read in preparation for reading a book and understanding the context from which the author speaks.

These are my favorite books and my favorite authors. Now I have an added awe and respect for them; one that I never had before I tried to write a book. As I sit here this afternoon with my treasure of books all around me, it is a strange sensation. I hear the various authors from different traditions and different time periods all speaking to one another and arguing their points of view. I think they would have all liked each other immensely...and had a great time at a party thrown in their honor. It seems to me that all these people cared about living a full life, a good life, and in sharing what they had learned with others.

My debt to all these people is great. I think back to the desire of mine to study so many different subjects, and I feel gratified that many of my life interests have been an integral part of my work with young children.

BIBLIOGRAPHY
Arbuthnot, May Hill. *Children and Books.* Chicago: Scott Foresman and Co., 1964.
Belgau, Frank. Web site: Balametrics.
Bessell, Harold and Uvaldo Palomares. *Methods in Human Development.* San Diego: Human Development Training Institute, 1967.
Bland, Jane Cooper. *Art of the Young Child.* New York: The Museum of Modern Art, 1968.
Collins, Marva and Civia Tamarkin. *Marva Collins' Way.* Los Angeles: J.P. Tarcher, 1990.
Comenius, John Amos. *The School of the Mother.* Chapel Hill: University of North Carolina Press, 1956.
Core Knowledge Preschool Sequence. Charlottesville, Virginia: Core Knowledge Foundation, 2000.
Doughton, Sudie Hunt. "Children's Preferences for Book Illustrations as Related to Age and Sex," Unpublished Master's Thesis. Knoxville: The University of Tennessee, 1964.

Ekstein, Rudolf and Rocco Motto. *From Learning for Love to Love of Learning, Essays on Psychoanalysis and Education.* New York: Bruner/Mazel Publishers, 1969.

Fabre, Jean-Henri, Linda Davis. *The Passionate Observer.* San Francisco: Chronicle Books, 1998.

Glasser, William. *Schools Without Failure.* New York: Harper and Row, 1969.

Goertzel, Victor and Mildred Goertzel. *Cradles of Eminence.* Boston: Little Brown, 1962.

Goodnow, Jacqueline. *Children Drawing.* Cambridge: Harvard University Press, 1977.

Hainstock, Elizabeth. *Teaching Montessori in the Home.* New York: Random House, 1968.

Hay, Julie, Charles Wingo. *Reading with Phonics, Teacher's Edition.* Philadelphia, J.B. Lippincott Company, 1954.

Hay, Julie, Charles Wingo, and Mary Hletko. *Reading with Phonics.* Philadelphia, J.B. Lippincott, 1967.

Highberger, Ruth. *Child Development for Day Care Workers.* Boston, et al: Houghton Mifflin Company, 1976.

Hirsch, E.D., Jr. *Cultural Literacy, What Every American Needs to Know.* Boston, et al: Houghton Mifflin Co., 1987.

_____ and John Holdren. What *Your Kindergartner Needs to Know.* New York: Dell Publishing, 1996.

Hymes, James. *Behavior and Misbehavior, a Teacher's Guide to Action.* Englewood Cliffs, N.J.: Prentice-Hall, Inc., 1958.

Jourard, Sidney. *Healthy Personality.* New York: Macmillan Co., 1974.

Kellog, Rhonda. *Analyzing Children's Art.* Palo Alto, California: National Press Books, 1969.

Kohn, Alfie. *Punished by Rewards.* New York: Houghton Mifflin Co., 1993.

Lair, Jess. *I Ain't Much Baby, But I'm All I've Got.* Bozeman, Montana, Unpublished mimeograph copy, 1969. This is now available as a Fawcett Crest Book.

Lillard, Charles and Terry Glavin. *A Voice Great Within Us.* Vancouver, Canada: New Star Books, 1998.

Lowenfeld, Viktor and W. Lambert Brittain. *Creative and Mental Growth, 5th Edition.* New York: The Macmillan Co., 1970

MacDonald, G. Jeffrey. "Montessori Looks Back and Ahead." *USA*

Bibliography

Today, Jan. 25, 2007.

Makar, Barbara. *Primary Phonics*, Sets 1-5, Sets M1 and M2. Cambridge, Massachusetts: Educators Publishing Service, Inc., 1977-1978.

McHugh, Helga. *Kindergarten, A Very Special Time and Place*. Missoula: Dept. of Home Economics, University of Montana, 1974.

Montessori, Maria. *The Discovery of the Child*. New York: Ballantine Books, 1967.

_____. *The Secret of Childhood*. New York: Ballantine Books, 1967.

_____. *The Absorbent Mind*. Madras, India: The Theosophical Publishing House, 1959.

Ong, Walter. *Orality and Literacy*. New York: Methuen, 1982.

Ota, Koshi, and others. *Printing for Fun*. New York: McDowell, Obolensky, 1960.

"Pat Carfra, The Lullaby Lady." *Times Colonist*. Victoria, B.C., Canada, May 20, 2003.

Peters, Marilyn Becker. *Paw Prints of the Tiger*. Nashville: ACW Press, 2006.

Pipher Mary. *Reviving Ophelia*. New York: Ballantine Books, 1995.

Raabe, Janis Asad. Phonics Practice Readers, Set 1, Short Vowels and Set 2, Long Vowels. Cleveland: Modern Curriculum Press, 1981.

Read, Katherine. *The Nursery School*. Philadelphia: W.B. Saunders Company, 1966.

Rodenburg, Patsy. *The Need for Words: Voice and Text*. London: Methuen Drama, 1993.

Rose, Anna. *Room for One More*. New York: Dell Publishing Company, Inc. 1969.

Rouma, Georges. *El lenguaje Grafico Del Nino*. Buenas Aires: Libreria y Editorial "El Ateneo," 1947.

Sassoon, Rosemary. *The Practical Guide to Children's Handwriting*. London: Thames and Hudson, 1983.

St. Nicholas Training Centre for the Montessori Method of Education. *External Diploma Course Tutor Guided*. London, United Kingdom: (not available except to students in the course)

Teachers of North Elementary School, Winston Salem, N.C. *1931-32 Within Our Cupboard,* North Elementary School. Unpublished, mimeograph copy, 1932.

Tan, Lesley. *Auditory Processing Series: No. 1 Behaviour, Communication and Auditory Processing, No.2 Auditory Processing at Home, 1998, No. 3 Audio Processing at School, 1999, No. 4 Auditory Processing and the Under Sixes, 2000.* Camberwell, Australia: Listening Works. (admin@listeningworks.com.au)

Viola, Wilhelm. *Child Art and Frank Cizek.* Vienna: Austrian Junior Red Cross, 1936. American Distributor: New York: The John Day Company.

Weaver, Richard. *Visions of Order.* Baton Rouge: Louisiana State University Press, 1964.

Wheelis, Allen. *The Quest for Identity.* New York: Norton, 1958.

White, Burton. *The First Three Years of Life.* Englewood Cliffs, N.J., Prentice Hall, 1984.

Wolf, Aline D. *Mommy, It's a Renoir!* Hollidaysburg, Pa.: Parent Child Press, 1984.

Zander, Rosamund and Benjamin Zander. *The Art of Possibility.* Boston: Harvard Business School Press, 2000.

Zinsser, William, and others. *Inventing the Truth, The Art and Craft of Memoir.* Boston, New York: The Houghton Mifflin Company, 1995.

IN CLOSING

    For many days and months I have gone over the material in this book. I have found something to improve each time. I'm sure I could read and reread and never really "finish." It is kind of scary to let go of it. But its real purpose is not to sit on my desk awaiting a better word here and there and a changed paragraph or two. It is to share the experiences, ideas, questions, etc. with my friends and family and other people who might be interested.

    I have a belief that not just the "good swimmers" should swim; not just the trained musicians should make music; not just the "good writers" should write, etc. I hope the meaning and ideas I want to convey are understandable. Please overlook and forgive any typos or misspellings or other errors I did not find and correct.

    Best wishes to each and every one of you, "my readers," and may God bless you in your endeavors and keep you safe in His care now and always.

SDM

Made in the USA